S0-CFJ-504

NOV - 8 1994

OCT 1 2

OCT 27/95

THE PSYCHOLOGY
OF INTERGROUP RELATIONS:
CONFLICT AND CONSCIOUSNESS

Psychology and the Problems of Society

Kenneth J. Gergen, Consulting Editor
Swarthmore College

Ashmore and McConahay:
Psychology and America's Urban Dilemmas

Kidder and Stewart:
The Psychology of Intergroup Relations
Conflict and Consciousness

Pizer and Travers:
Psychology and Social Change

THE PSYCHOLOGY OF INTERGROUP RELATIONS: CONFLICT AND CONSCIOUSNESS

Louise H. Kidder
Temple University

V. Mary Stewart
York University

McGraw-Hill Book Company

New York/St. Louis/San Francisco/Düsseldorf/Johannesburg
Kuala Lumpur/London/Mexico/Montreal/New Delhi/Panama
Paris/São Paulo/Singapore/Sydney/Tokyo/Toronto

To D. T. C., R. L. K., J. P. L., and P. S.
for their unobtrusive but not unfelt influence

The Psychology of Intergroup Relations
Conflict and Consciousness

Copyright © 1975 by McGraw-Hill, Inc. All rights reserved.
Printed in the United States of America. No part of this publication
may be reproduced, stored in a retrieval system, or transmitted, in any
form or by any means, electronic, mechanical, photocopying, recording, or
otherwise, without the prior written permission of the publisher.

234567890   BPBP   798765

This book was set in Press Roman by Allen Wayne Technical
Corp. The editor was Richard R. Wright;
the cover was designed by J. E. O'Connor;
the cover illustration by Cathy Hull;
the production supervisor was Milton J. Heiberg.
The Book Press, Inc., was printer and binder.

HM
133
K45

ERINDALE
COLLEGE
LIBRARY

Library of Congress Cataloging in Publication Data

Kidder, Louise H
    The psychology of intergroup relations.

    (Psychology and the problems of society)
    1. Social groups. 2. Prejudices and antipathies.
3. Social perceptions. I. Stewart, Mary, date
joint author. II. Title. [DNLM: 1. Prejudice.
2. Psychology, Social. 3. Racial relations. HM251
K46p]
HM133.K45   301.18'028   74-10985
ISBN 0-07-034545-7

Acknowledgments

The authors wish to acknowledge here the following material used with permission from other sources:

E. Durkheim, *Suicide,* © 1951, Macmillan Publishing Co., N.Y.

F. M. Solomon et al., "Civil Rights Activity and Reduction of Crime Among Negroes," in *Archives of General Psychiatry,* Copyright 1965, American Medical Association.

E. Cleaver, *Soul on Ice,* © 1968, McGraw-Hill Book Co., N.Y.

Black Rage, by William H. Grier and Price M. Cobbs, © 1968 by William H. Grier and Price M. Cobbs, Basic Books, Inc., Publishers, New York.

E. Berscheid and E. H. Walster, *Interpersonal Attraction,* © 1969. Addison-Wesley Publishing Co., Reading, Mass.

"Sex Equality: The Beginnings of Ideology," by Alice S. Rossi, *The Humanist,* Sept./Oct. 1969.

"Gay Is Good for Us All," by Suzannah Lessard, *The Washington Monthly,* December 1970, Copyright by *The Washington Monthly.*

Waubageshig, *The Only Good Indian,* © 1970, New Press, Toronto, Canada.

"Is Woman's Liberation a Lesbian Plot?" by Sidney Abbott and Barbara Love, in *Woman in Sexist Society,* © 1971, by Basic Books Inc., Publishers, New York.

J. Ransom Arthur, *An Introduction to Social Psychology,* © J. Ransom Arthur, 1971.

Contents

answer

Foreword

During the critical moments of recent social history, great discontent with the behavioral sciences has often been voiced. Why, it is lamented, did the sciences not forsee our present plight, why do they have no trustworthy solutions to our dilemmas? We face economic depression, world war, internal revolutions, chaos in government, rampant poverty, bitter antagonisms among groups—and the behavioral scientists seem to respond with empty words. The problems are immediate and painful, and the scientist drones on endlessly with abstractions that seem infinitely removed from reality. We want action and we get conjecture.

The authors of the present volume, Louise Kidder and Mary Stewart, were both graduate students in psychology during one of the most bitter periods of American history. The engagement of the United States in the Vietnam War had rent the nation at its very core; social revolution was afoot; the cry for action was everywhere. Kidder and Stewart were deeply invested in these issues and did not wish to see their professional careers grow increasingly remote from such concerns. Rather, it was their intent to bring about a thorough integration of their career pursuits and their concern with critical social issues. The present volume on intergroup relations is a salutary outgrowth of this attempt. Seldom have I encountered a document in the behavioral sciences that so effectively transforms scientific abstractions into vital insights and incentives for concerted action. Suddenly the words have been brought to life and the implications are indeed profound.

The volume itself is divided into five chapters, each elaborating a major thesis that is stated at the beginning. The initial chapter cogently argues that all accounts of intergroup relations are biased; all contain implicit values, errors, and distortions. Kidder and Stewart show how the behavioral scientist attempts to avoid many of these biases, but their candor is truly refreshing when they conclude not only that such attempts are not wholly successful but also that their own account is biased as well. The second chapter delves headlong into a major source of group conflict: the process by which people compare themselves with one another. Particular attention is given to the role of dissimilarity in driving people apart. Needs for self-esteem are also singled out for their strong contribution to intergroup hostility, an argument which has profound implications for Western culture where esteem needs are so often fulfilled at others' expense.

Chapter 3 examines the central role played by competition—that old American ideal—in fostering hatred between groups. After showing that the actual outcomes are far less significant to people in determining their satisfaction than relative outcomes, the authors delve into the issue of colonialism. We often view colonialism as a thing of the past; however, Kidder and Stewart show that present-day exploitation of minority groups is fundamentally similar to it. This discussion leads naturally into a treatment, in the following chapter, of social power and the process of social labeling. What a person is called may well determine his or her social fate.

In the final chapter the authors move from the theoretical to the practical. Given the exploitation of certain groups by others, what can be done? In the present volume radical rhetoric is replaced by reason and factual documentation. The pros and cons of various alternatives are explored, with the final hope raised for widespread social change stemming from a union among groups.

This is inspired behavioral science and may hopefully encourage others to dare as well.

Kenneth J. Gergen
Professor and Chairman
Department of Psychology
Swarthmore College

Preface

Titles sometimes promise something more or other than they deliver; that is why we wish to use this opportunity to show our respect for the truth-in-packaging principle by telling the reader just what to expect. This short book attempts to introduce the reader to some classic and modern studies and theories concerning the age-old problem of prejudice. We did not want to entitle our volume *Prejudice,* for Gordon Allport got there first in 1954 with his excellent book by that name. Nor did we wish to focus exclusively on ethnic and racial prejudice with the specificity and detail of Allport's approach. Instead, our goal was to view prejudice as one of the reprehensible but persistent side-effects of a number of social-psychological phenomena.

As our first chapter points out, all investigators have their biases, and we are no exception. Rather than offering abstract definitions of our points of view, we shall give the reader some information about our pasts, which has determined our perspectives. The authors are both white Anglo-Saxon Protestant females, which might seem to be an immediate disqualification for writing a book on prejudice; however, each of us has stepped out of the mainstream at various points to work and live in Zambia and South India, to become acquainted with the women's movement, and to live in a Christian commune and an intentional community. Each of us also studied social psychology at Northwestern University, and the influence of the social psychologists there appears throughout the book. We shall stop reminiscing here, with the hope that this conveys something of the flavor and perspective to come.

We have made an attempt to go beyond our own ethnocentric perspectives by introducing material from other lands and cultures. Our experience of living and working in India and Africa has convinced us that prejudice rears its ugly head not only in America. However, in spite of our attempts to include non-American material given the universality of intergroup conflict, the reader will quickly notice

that references to North American black-white and male-female relations predominate. This emphasis reflects the fact that these two topics
figure heavily in the literature and that they hit closest to home. The
reader who would like to investigate further the problems of prejudice
in other lands and among other groups can find such cross-cultural
material in a recent book by LeVine and Campbell (1972) entitled
Ethnocentrism.

    To these claims and disclaimers we must add another. We do not
include labor-management relations or international wrangles in our
study of intergroup relations since these are conflicts in which the
groups, the rules, and the bargaining tools are already well-defined and
structured, and which operate according to different laws. The reader
interested in such rule structures will find a stimulating set of readings
by Brickman (1974) entitled *Social Conflict.* The intergroup conflict
and consciousness that we discuss arise in situations that have no
built-in mechanisms for negotiation. What we attempt to show is the
process by which such intergroup relations are socially defined and
negotiated in the first place, and the manner in which change subsequently occurs as a result of the group's awareness that things can
indeed be negotiated.

    If we do hit close to home, we hope that we do not in the process
hit the reader over the head too often. We all have strong feelings and
biases with regard to certain social issues and, as we explain in our
book, our values are bound to show. We ask the reader to bear with
us if our feelings are sometimes poorly hidden. These occasional raw
edges may serve as reminders of the major bruises that social groups
have inflicted on one another. And they may also serve another purpose—if we may make a most immodest claim—that of contributing to
the collective consciousness.

    Finally, lest we leave the reader with the impression that we did
all this with our own heads and hands alone, we would like to acknowledge the advice and assistance of the following persons. Erasmus
Hoch, Dave Kenny, Dave Kipnis, and Neil McGuffin all read and
commented on the entire manuscript. We took their comments to
heart and put their advice into print, yet, while some of the credit is
theirs, the responsibility for the flaws that remain is still ours. Sandy
Candeub, Donna DiFurio, and Evi Holland provided the secretarial and
organizational skills needed to put the manuscript together. And, last,

we thank two persons who really came in at the beginning—Ken Gergen and Phil Brickman initially proposed that we write this book, and without their early encouragement and ideas this might still be a dream rather than a reality.

Louise H. Kidder
V. Mary Stewart

Chapter 1

Studies of Groups: Values in Science and Culture

PROPOSITION

Anyone who writes or tells you a story does so from a particular perspective, with a particular set of values, errors, and distortions. Social scientists have rules and resources to fight this tendency, but they can never be completely free from it. In this chapter we examine the sources of bias from theoretical, methodological and ethical perspectives.

Illustrative Work

If you ever played the parlor game of Telephone, you know how messages get garbled in transmission. Each person hears and sends a revised version of the message, so that what started out as "John has pretty red hair" becomes "John is pretty red," which becomes "John is embarrassed," (or, "John is a Marxist"), and so on.

Science also involves a form of serial transmission—messages must travel from the external source to the scientist's receptors, to his associative centers, and through a web of past associations, all of which add noise and tend to garble the message. If physical scientists have problems, social scientists sometimes face real dilemmas, because the source of many of their messages is often once removed from the event—another person is telling them about an event. And as soon as we listen to one person tell his side of a story, we must recognize that there is another person who could tell us the other side. This is especially true of studies in intergroup relations, where there are obviously two or more sides and each may accuse the other of being biased. Ironically, we have often failed to realize that there was more than one side until someone called out "bias!" (Becker, 1967). Until students began asking for black history courses, for example, teachers had not thought of the standard courses as particularly "white." Until researchers began doing sociological work from the deviant's point of view (Becker, 1963), scholars had not thought of the standard sociology as being particularly "straight."

Social psychologists have been particularly aware of the potential for bias, for good social psychological reasons underlie it. There are *theoretical* and *methodological* grounds for systematic distortions in perception (e.g., Allport & Postman, 1947; Bruner, 1957). There are also theoretical and methodological reasons for our blind spots, for our not being aware of our own biases. In the pages which follow, we shall present the theoretical, methodological, and ethical issues or *problems* of bias in research, followed by our suggested *solutions* for each of these areas.

Theoretical Issues   In Gardner Murphy's prose:

> We do not really see with our eyes or hear with our ears. If we all saw with our eyes, we would see pretty much alike. We should differ only so far as retinal structure, eyeball structure, *etc.*, differ. We differ much more widely than this because we see not only with our eyes, but also with our midbrain, our visual and associative centers, and with our systems of incipient behavior, to which almost all visual perceiving leads (1947, p. 333).

Yet what perceiver thinks of this as he looks at a rose, or studies a child, or researches race relations? We are all true believers in the factuality of our perceptions, and take them as given truths (Campbell, 1967, 1969; Segall, Campbell, & Herskovits, 1966). Thus, when ten black writers

(Clark, 1968) accused William Styron, a white southerner, of giving a biased account of Nat Turner's slave revolt (1966), they did not write their accounts with the same apologies or tentativeness that Styron should have used. They wrote with the conviction that they were right. Continual tentativeness or humble apologies for errors in our judgments would paralyze, so we barge ahead with confidence.

This is not to say that our scientific "facts" are really fantasies. The closer we adhere to the rules of evidence and procedures of experimentation, the more error-free our observations are likely to be. And unlike the rules of poetry or fiction, the methods of science require that we check our observations against the external world, so that at least the events which we describe are relatively undisputed. Even William Styron and the ten black writers agreed on certain gross facts—Nat Turner led a slave revolt and he had a vision. It is only in the more subtle interpretations of these facts that disagreements arise. While Styron describes Nat Turner's vision as a hallucination of the angel Gabriel, the ten black writers describe it as a vision of a new world of freedom.

The following table shows where the disagreement often lies:

Table 1-1

| | | Facts or Traits (Denotations) | |
		Trait X	Opposite of X
Evaluations of the facts or traits (Connotations)	Positive	Open, friendly (A's description of self)	Reserved (B's description of self)
	Negative	Bumptious, brash (B's description of A)	Cold, closed (A's description of B)

(Adapted from Campbell, 1967, p. 822).

Both A and B agree that they differ on the trait dimension: that is, when each describes the other, they keep the descriptions denotatively correct, staying in the same columns, but they attribute opposite connotations, with negative overtones. Britishers call Americans "bumptious" or "brash" while Americans reciprocate with labels like "cold" or "closed."

An example of the pot calling the kettle black among social scientists with different perspectives is given by Bem (1970). He points out that a researcher with obvious political biases did a study of the "love of life" among the supporters of Eugene McCarthy, Richard Nixon, Hubert Humphrey, and George Wallace (Maccoby, 1968). Maccoby found that 77 percent of the McCarthy supporters were "life-lovers," "attracted to that which is alive, which grows, which is free and unpredictable" while 80 percent of the Wallace supporters fell at the opposite pole, "attracted to that which is rigidly ordered, mechanical, and unalive" (p. 2). As Bem points out, Maccoby chose to call his two groups "life-lovers" and "antilifers." A researcher with different political persuasions could just as well have named them "bleeding-heart anarchists" and "pragmatic realists," respectively. These two descriptions agree on the trait dimension and disagree on the evaluative dimension:

Table 1-2

| | | Traits | |
		Trait X	Opposite of X
Evaluations	Positive	Maccoby: McCarthy supporters are "life-lovers"	Other researchers: Wallace supporters are "pragmatic realists"
	Negative	Other researchers: McCarthy supporters are "bleeding-heart anarchists"	Maccoby: Wallace supporters are "antilifers"

Christie and Jahoda (1954) have compiled similar criticisms of the work and theory in *The Authoritarian Personality* (Adorno, et al., 1950). Written at a time when the world was shaken by the horrors of the Nazi scapegoating of Jews, some persons found a new scapegoat of sorts—the authoritarian. The authoritarian personality was anti-Semitic, acquiescent, rigid, intolerant of ambiguity, and politically right wing. Critics of this work have asked, Is it not possible that there might also be other people who are anti-Semitic, acquiescent, rigid, intolerant of ambiguity, and politically left wing? Or even liberal (Brown, 1951; Rokeach, 1961; Shils, 1954)?

Historical and anthropological accounts of intergroup relations also demonstrate the influence an investigator's perspective or allegiance has on his findings. Two accounts of the Mau Mau in Kenya say rather different things about the Kikuyu's feelings about their land and the European's place on it.

From Majdalany (1963), who collected accounts from white settlers and British officials, we hear:

> The Kikuyu has a mystical attachment to his land. It is something sacred and deeply involved in his religious observance. Any dispute over land is therefore not amenable to reason or logic or equity in the European sense of these terms, and this again makes rational negotiation in land problems virtually impossible (p. 29).

From Kariuki (1964), who was a member of the movement (called Mau Mau by its opponents), we hear another version reported from one of Kenyatta's speeches:

> He said that he did not want the Europeans to leave the country, but it was time that they started to behave like guests in our house. . . . They should not forget that the land they tread is ours (p. 11).

Both agree on the importance of the land to the Kikuyu people, but while the accounts from white settlers speak somewhat patronizingly of an irrational "mystical attachment" to the land, the Kikuyu writer quite bluntly and unmystically warns that the Europeans "not forget that the land they tread is ours."

A similar case of two sides of the story is the British versus the Indian version of the Sepoy "mutiny" of 1857. *The Cambridge History of India* (Dodwell, 1932) says:

> The incident that precipitated the Mutiny is known to all the world. . . . A [Brahman feared he] would soon lose his caste, for cartridges, greased with the fat of cows or swine were being manufactured by the government, and every Sepoy would be obliged to bite them before loading his rifle. It needs a sympathetic imagination to gauge the shock under which the mind of the Brahman reeled (p. 173).

An Indian writer (Savarkas, 1947), on the other hand, describes the revolt not as a mutiny, but as a war of independence, started not by a Brahman's superstitious fears but by the unrest of a nation subjected to colonialism.

Different versions of the same events come not only from interested partisans; they appear also in the work of disinterested third parties. Compare the interpretations made by non-Kwakiutl writers of the Kwakiutl potlatch, a ritual in which each person tries to outdo his neighbor in lavishly giving away his possessions. While some describe it as a vengeful act of near-war—a kind of. overkill through overgive (e.g., Codere, 1950, Rohner & Rohner, 1970)—at least one (Mauss, 1954) has described it more as gift giving. The excesses (throwing a year's supply of cooking fuel into the sea; burning one's house; giving away valuable copper articles) are not expressions of vengeance but of sacrifice. And burning one's home is not a way of saying to a rival, "See if you can match this," but rather a way of saying to the gods, "See how much I care."

If trained social scientists have difficulty seeing their data from another perspective, or even recognizing that theirs is but a limited point of view, it is no wonder that laymen err. Bronfenbrenner (1961) shows how reciprocal distortions of one another have hurt Soviet-American relations—each, assuming that the other is devious, interprets even friendly gestures as tricks. White (1966) suggests that we continue to have war among nations that want to avoid it because each side fails to read the mind of the other. And rival football teams have diametrically opposed definitions of which side played rough and "dirty" (Hastorf & Cantril, 1954).

Raymond Gorden (unpublished) has developed ways of *training* people, if not to read the minds of others, at least to learn how others think of particular events. He has devised training materials for prospective Peace Corps volunteers and crosscultural travelers so that they may see them. His tape-recorded minidramas with musical sound effects depict communication breakdowns between North Americans and Latin Americans. One set of tapes presents a scene in which a North American tries to cash a check in a Colombian bank and goes out fuming because the Colombians behind him elbow their way in front of him at the teller's window while he waits for his cash. He commiserates with other Peace Corps volunteers, concluding that Colombians do not know how to stand in line, and "Sometimes I wonder whether these Colombians are civilized yet!" The scene changes, and to give us the Colombian side of the story, a Colombian interviewer approaches the bank teller and asks what kind of customers the North Americans are. The teller says: "They are rude. . . . They hand their check to me and then stand right in front of the window until they get their cash. . . . and it makes many of the customers angry!" The Colombian interviewer leaves, satisfied that she knows what the problem is. But naïve North Americans listening to this recording are still puzzled—What is wrong with waiting in front of the window until you get your cash? To finish the story, Gorden has a North American interview the Colombian interviewer, and we finally learn that in Colombia

> . . . the customer goes to the window, hands the check to the teller, steps back away from the window so that others give their checks to the teller, and then when his check is approved for cashing, the teller will call his name.

Moreover, bank customers do not form a line ". . . because it would make the system much less efficient."

The North Americans were right—Colombians do not stand in line at the bank. And the Colombians were right—North Americans do not step aside to wait their turn. But each was wrong in interpreting the other's behavior as rude or pushy. The objective facts were correct, but the evaluative interpretations were amiss. Only by hearing the Colombian's version of what happened could the North American listener appreciate his interpretive error. (And a Colombian, likewise, would benefit from hearing the North American's version if he anticipated banking in the United States.) Some paper-and-pencil methods and measures of such perspectival training are also being developed (e.g., Fiedler et al., 1971; Foa et al., 1971) to be used as "culture assimilators."

Such minidrama techniques can not only turn fresh Peace Corps volunteers into good visitors but also make social scientists aware of the fact that there are at least two sides to every story of intergroup relations. Ideally, a researcher should do as the tape recordings do—listen to what A says about an event, then interview B about the same event, and finally confront one interpretation with the other to uncover the diver-

gent assumptions behind each. The following section on methodological
issues examines some of the problems an investigator encounters along
the way.

Methodological Issues   There seems to be a "hierarchy of credibility"
(Becker, 1967) which makes superordinates more believable than subordinates, the straight world more trustworthy than the deviant world,
possibly men more credible than women (Goldberg, 1968), and whites
more credible than blacks. So if an interviewer gathers the opinions of
janitors, drug addicts, housewives, or black students on issues of concern to each group, he is likely to be accused of being biased and not
objective. Becker (1967) concludes that in organizational settings, where
superordinates call subordinates' viewpoints biased, the problem is insoluble: If the interviewer tries to appease that set of superordinates by
listening to their side, then *their* superordinates feel threatened and make
the same accusations. Every boss has a boss and, conversely, every
underling an underling, as Gouldner (1968) points out. It becomes a
problem of infinite regress—the investigator is damned if he does and
damned if he doesn't interview the next group in line.

If vertical hierarchies present a dilemma, there is a horizontal analogue among groups that differ on racial, sexual, religious, or other
social dimensions. An entire issue of a journal has been devoted to the
problem of "The White Researcher in Black Society" (Clark, 1973).
While the black contributors have focused on what we have called
theoretical and ethical issues, a white contributor emphasized his own
methodological problem of gaining entry and trust (Couchman, 1973).
He noted that the group of men whom he wanted to interview had been
interviewed previously by another group of white researchers and they
did not take kindly to the interpretations or publicity of those research
efforts. In this respect, a black psychologist may have won their trust
and confidence more readily. The author goes on to note, however, that
skin color alone does not create or solve all problems of entry. He found
that, within a single neighborhood, some persons were alienated by his
use of the term *Negro,* while others were equally upset by his reference
to *black;* presumably a black researcher would have faced the same
problems in his choice of words.

Several contributors to the journal also note that the problem lies
not so much with white researchers as with white *research* in black

society, and black as well as white psychologists may be carriers of the latter (e.g., Brazziel, 1973). Much depends upon the psychologist's training. If he employs inappropriate measures based on white norms and white experiences, he stacks the cards against both the accuracy of his research and the favorableness which his conclusions reflect on his respondents.

Kenneth Clark, a black psychologist and former president of the American Psychological Association, discovered in his own work in Harlem (1965) that

> . . . the use of standardized questionnaires and interview procedures would result in stylized and superficial verbal responses or evasions. The . . . data obtained by these traditional methods did not plumb the depth or the complexities of the attitudes and anxieties, the many forms of irony and rage which form the truths of the lives of the people of Harlem (p. xix).

Thus, a black researcher, armed with traditional white-oriented measures, may come no closer to the truth than his similarly armed white counterpart.

Another writer explains how tests which are obviously based on white norms and patterns of culture may elicit distorted answers from black respondents. With IQ tests in particular, he points out, black students probably feel anxious, angry, and resentful over the content of the tests, which implies that knowledge of white formal culture constitutes "intelligence."

> They ask questions about things like the distance from Boston to London, how to keep from being lost in the wilderness, the author of Macbeth, the cause of icebergs melting, and such. They ask for the definition of words which are much more frequently used in white than in black culture (Jorgensen, 1973, p. 35).

A white Northeasterner asked to estimate the distance between Tuskegee and Tougaloo or to name the author of *Black Skin, White Masks* would be similarly disadvantaged.

White researchers in white society likewise have no guarantees of easy access or accurate reporting. When John Dollard (1937) a Northern white psychologist, attempted to interview Southerners, he reported that he encountered fewer problems with Southern black respondents than with Southern whites, for the *whites* distrusted this *Yankee* and feared that he felt holier than they.

Earlier work on the problem of bias introduced by various interviewer characteristics found that the information which interviewers obtain is likely to be tainted by their sex, age, race, or social class (e.g., Athey et al., 1960; Cantril, 1944; Benney et al., 1956; Katz, 1942). Now we realize that controlling for the characteristics alone may not be the end of our task, for we need to inquire into the researcher's values, measures, and biases regardless of his external attributes. We shall treat these issues in further detail both in the following section on the *ethical* issues and in the latter part of the chapter on methodological and ethical *solutions.*

One solution to the problem of interviewer effects is to rely not upon one or two interviewers but to treat *interviewer* as a factor in the research, and have three of four interviewers in each racial-sexual-religious-economic-political category so that all salient characteristics are methodologically controlled for. Such controls are costly and may tend to be regarded as luxuries in research design. In the delicate areas of intergroup relations, however, we would be well advised to reckon with them, for here are sources of bias that we *know* exist and that we *can* control.

Ethical Issues   The existence of bias and systematic errors in social science presents not only theoretical and methodological problems, but also ethical concerns. Even the most abstract basic research has social-policy implications and may be put to use some day. Like Einstein, whose theories found tragic uses, the social scientist is in some sense responsible for the ends to which his discoveries are ultimately put.

There are obvious policy implications to many of the questions social scientists ask, and the questions themselves are often unintentionally loaded. A psychologist who asks, "What are the *personality* factors underlying student unrest?" is likely to make very different policy recommendations from one who asks, "What are the *social* conditions underlying student unrest?" (Sawyer, 1970a). While the former may recommend special counseling or child-rearing practices to eliminate unrest, the latter is more likely to recommend a redistribution of income or an end to military conscription.

Similarly loaded questions have been asked about the causes of ghetto "riots." Let us compare the *riff-raff* explanation of riots with the *blocked-opportunity* theory. The former implies that riots occur because uneducated unruly persons in the populace have nothing better to do than to stir up trouble. The latter suggests that there are *real*, justifiable causes for rioting, and the difference between persons who riot and those who do not lies not in their personalities but in their perception and experience of racial discrimination. A study that compared the evidence for each of these explanations found no data to support the personality-centered notions (or at least not for the presumed personality orientation since, if anything, the persons who participated in riots were *better* educated and *better* informed than those who did not). But the study did find abundant support for the system-centered blocked-opportunity theory (Caplan & Paige, 1968). The policy implications of these two different approaches are drastically different. The personality-centered approach may suggest either counseling the disgruntled population to eliminate their anger or, if that fails, institutionalizing them, thereby physically removing the threat. The system-centered approach, on the other hand, would suggest eliminating the obstacles to equal opportunity, which means not only opening the doors of jobs and schools but also arranging the programs within those doors to ensure an equal chance of success or survival.

Perhaps most problematic of all for scientists is their tendency to remain relatively unaware of the diverse policy implications that their research may have. Some recent controversial work on the relative contributions of heredity and environment to IQ scores reveals this dilemma. On the one hand, Arthur Jensen's work on the heritability of intelligence is often used to argue that compensatory education is useless (e.g., Jensen, 1969). His work has been amply criticized by other psychologists who point out that the data that Jensen used provide a poor test of the hypothesis and do not present so strong a case for inheritance (e.g., Hunt, 1969; Kagan, 1969). We subscribe to the critics' views and encourage the reader to pursue their arguments. On the other hand, we could also make a strong argument *in favor of* the utility of compensatory education, using some of Jensen's own conclusions.

Let us assume for the moment that socioeconomic status and success (often abbreviated SES) in the United States are related not to IQ scores but to ping-pong playing ability. (The actual relation between SES and IQ scores is not very strong according to Jencks et al. 1972). Suppose further that genetic factors contribute to ping-pong-playing ability. One policy implication might be that we should close all ping-pong-playing schools and let our fate rest with our genes. The opposite implication, however, is just as plausible. If ping-pong playing is a necessary skill in America and the highest salaries and finest homes belong to ping-pong champions, this could provide all the more reason for establishing educational programs and practice facilities for persons not so endowed.

This fantasy[1] is not intended to affirm the claims of persons who believe that races, nations, or tribes differ in their genetic endowments. It is intended rather to show that if there are *individual* differences in heritable skills or attributes, we can try to compensate for such inequalities by providing social benefits. Thus, instead of a do-nothing social policy, we might institute a reform policy to ensure everyone equal access to the finest homes, highest salaries, most desirable jobs, or whatever other rewards accompany outstanding performance.

Yet a third alternative, of course, would be to abolish the game of ping-pong, or any other activity, as a basis for economic success and instead allocate incomes equally. This solution is preferred by these authors and advocated by Jencks et al. (1972), but a full consideration of it lies outside the scope of this book.

We have deliberately used something as silly as ping-pong in our example in order to raise yet another ethical problem. One of the conceptual limitations of "majority-group" research is its tendency to regard divergences from the majority group's norm as signs of *deviance* rather than simply of *difference* (Gordon, 1973). Deviations from white IQ norms are regarded as failings rather than as different ways of responding to the questions. Deviations from white family patterns are regarded as "weak" or "unstable" rather than simply as alternative structures. Were we to approach the white middle-class family with a different set of values, we might find, much to our dismay, that the father is *absent* for all practical purposes (Seeley et al., 1956) because he is gone ten or twelve hours of the day and, when at home, wants to be left alone to relax, read the paper, and watch his favorite programs. Is this any better or worse than a family in which the father is home

---

[1] We owe the origin of this fantasy to Howard S. Becker of Northwestern University who, in a seminar on utopias, made a similar case for (or against) rewarding the best ping-pong player in the United States with a $100,000 salary, a chauffer-driven car, and all the goods money could buy.

much of the day or absent altogether? True, the former family is richer and the latter poorer on the average, but is this our criterion for a "stable" or "strong" family?

The biases inherent in the evaluations attached to deviations from a majority group's norms are not so obvious when we use marriage, family, or IQ scores as examples. We have all been so trained to think that an IQ score of 130 is better rather than different from an IQ score of 90 that we do not stop to reflect on what this means. Like the family example, we might turn this one around to pity the conformist who scored 130 and praise the free thinker who scored 90. Once again, however, it is likely that the person who scores 130 will end up in a higher level job with a higher salary than will his lower-scoring peer. And again we should ask ourselves if this be a criterion or necessary consequence of what we mean by "intelligence."

The types of questions we ask may influence not only the kinds of policy recommendations we make but even our ability to foresee social changes. Industrial psychologists who studied the productivity and personalities of factory workers in the early 1930s found no hint of impending unionization because they were not asking questions related to that possibility (Homans, 1950). Similarly, most of the work on prejudice and race relations done in the 1950s could not predict the rise of black nationalism or the emergence of Stokely Carmichael. Most of that research dealt with the attitudes of white residents toward black neighbors (e.g., Deutsch & Collins, 1958), or white salesmen toward black customers (e.g., Saenger & Gilbert, 1950), or white workers toward black colleagues (Mackenzie, 1948). These are important issues and should not have been neglected, but the other side was relatively ignored. With few exceptions (e.g., Bayton, 1941; Mann, 1959; Roberts, 1953), social scientists did not inquire as much about the attitudes of black Americans toward whites. We knew little of a scientific nature about the attitudes of black people (cf. Pettigrew, 1964), just as we know little today about the attitudes of women. Both the Black Power movement (see Carmichael & Hamilton, 1967) and the women's liberation movement (see Friedan, 1963) thus came as rude shocks to the general public, and indeed there is little evidence that social scientists were prepared for these changes (though Kenneth Clark's work contains the seeds of predictions of black rage and rebellions—e.g., Clark, 1944; Clark & Barker, 1945; Clark, 1965).

Our earlier discussion of the theoretical and methodological sources of bias shows why these questions have not been asked. Since social science up to this time has been the occupation primarily of white, middle-class males, social scientists may understandably have had difficulty gaining access to, and valid information from, the unwhite, unmiddle-class, and unmale (cf. Chapter 5), and they may have only occasionally formulated their questions from an *unstatus quo* perspective (Sawyer, 1970b).

Possible Solutions to Problems of Bias

Lest we sound like prophets of doom, let us turn to a brighter side of the social-science picture with a look at some promising solutions to the theoretical, methodological, and ethical problems of bias.

Approaches to the Theoretical Issues An evolutionary approach puts the problem of error nicely in perspective. Campbell (1970, 1972) argues that scientific theories are subject to the same types of natural-selection pressures as species, instincts, and habits. The rules and rituals of science, moreover, hasten the process of selection, so that experiments weed out ill-fitting theories faster than if we let nature take its course. By continually subjecting our hypotheses to tests in the external world, we intensify the process of reality-testing, which works (but slowly) also on religious and common-sense knowledge. These external checks help keep our science honest and weed out those theories that are grounded more in the scientist's fancy than in fact.

One corollary of this argument is that the only good theory is an *old* theory, one that has stood the test of time, and modern science occasionally does vindicate ancient "superstitions." Fairly recently, for instance, medical researchers *discovered* that ephedrine, an extract from a Chinese herb used to treat respiratory ailments for about five thousand years, is a useful treatment for asthma (Shibutani, 1966, p. 161). This scientific affirmation, added to five thousand years of less rigorous testing, makes us very confident in this bit of knowledge, but we still allow for the possibility that a new religion or new scientific discovery may prove it wrong. The even more recent interest shown by the Western world in acupuncture is another case in point.

If we adhere to the rules of experimentation and subject our theories to tests against the external environment, replications by other scientists, and the predictions of competing theories, we may say that the theories which survive such selection pressures are "the best of the current year," and then continue to update our work (Campbell, 1970). The records are not nearly so neat because no one keeps a systematic score-card of the status of competing theories, but reviews of the literature (e.g., Amir, 1969) try at least to tally the outcomes and are the best index we have of the state of the field at any one time.

Approaches to the Methodological Issues   As long as we know what the sources of experimenter-induced errors are, we can do something to correct them. As pointed out earlier, if the interviewer's race, religion, sex, age, dress, and social class affect the answers he or she receives, then one solution is to take into account all demonstrably relevant variables and use interviewers of all descriptions as shown in Table 1-3.

Table 1-3   Interviewer Factors

Sex	Race	Social Class	Number
Male	Black	Middle	2
		Lower	2
	White	Middle	2
		Lower	2
Female	Black	Middle	2
		Lower	2
	White	Middle	2
		Lower	2

Finding sixteen interviewers (if we want the minimum of two in each of the eight cells) who fit these qualifications is difficult and costly, hence seldom done. But we know, at least, what we can do if we think these factors are salient and biasing.

A similar approach may handle the problem of gaining *access* to social groups or respondents. Ideally we would want each of the sixteen interviewers to approach sixteen different respondents who also fit each of the categories above, so that we could look for the effects of both *respondents'* sex, race, and social class and *interviewers'* sex, race, and social class. If, however, a white lower class male interviewer cannot get his foot in the door to interview a black middle-class female (or vice versa), we could at least hope to obtain interviews with each type of respondent by sending a matching interviewer. There is some evidence that persons speak more frankly with others who are like themselves or who are at least "wise" to their condition (Goffman, 1963). This matching technique has its drawbacks, however, for if we found differences we would not know whether they were due to the interviewers' or the respondents' characteristics. If we could make some nonmatched pairs (by having females interview males as well as females, and vice versa) we could begin to analyze the information obtained.

Faced with the cost or unavailability of sixteen interviewers to fit the eight categories, a researcher might be tempted to find interviewers who were neutral or could "pass" as different people in different settings. Such a plan could become either grotesque (with men passing as women, for instance), or painful (for the person who is "passing" and has the problem of information control and disclosure—Goffman, 1963). For persons who are genuinely "marginal men" (Park, 1950; Stonequist, 1937), the problems are no less serious; they are often members of neither group, suspected and rejected by both.

The methodological problems of experimenter-induced bias are complex, indeed, but not insoluble. There are at least recommendations and guidelines to follow.

Approaches to the Ethical Issues One approach to the problem of biased perspectives is to be *aware* that the problem exists. Two social scientists urge such awareness, one asking us to answer the question "Whose side are we on?" (Becker, 1967), the other advocating ". . . a psychology with conscious values" (Sawyer, 1970b). These advocates point out the following:

> Value-free science is a myth that serves the *status quo*. To deny that value decisions are involved is to let them be made largely in accord with established values. This may be particularly clear with military psychology. But other areas of psychology are not that different. . . . Persons who favor *status quo* values cannot hide behind a mythical cloak of scientific neutrality (Sawyer, 1970b, pp. 13–14).

and:

> . . . the question is not whether we should take sides, since we inevitably will, but rather whose side we are on. (Becker, 1967, p. 239).

It would seem to follow from such awareness that we should have social scientists of many persuasions studying the same issues, each stating with whom he sides and making his values known. (The authors of this book have made an effort in this direction by telling you in the preface *who* we are if not whose side we are on.) Davidoff (1965) describes such an advocate system within policy-making bodies of urban planners. This would provide us with a set of competing perspectives and remove the "cloak of scientific neutrality" which hides the problem now.

Some people would argue, however, that this is only the first step toward a solution. We should not only make ourselves aware of the value choices; we should *do* something about them. Gouldner (1968) speaks of making a commitment to eliminate human suffering:

> . . . one possible meaning of objectivity in social science is the contribution it might make to a human unity of mankind. But to make such a contribution the social sciences cannot and should not be impartial toward human suffering; they must not make their peace with any form of human unity that complacently accommodates itself to or imposes suffering (p. 116).

Having said this, we turn the problem over to the readers, the potential social scientists, advocates, problem solvers. Each can provide only his own answer to the question "Whose side are we on?" and make his own decision of what to *do*.

Unanswered Questions

In order to have people with varying perspectives doing social science research, we will have to recruit those having perspectives that are not yet included. Will we be able to attract and keep such persons within the field? Social psychological experiments on conformity show what happens to deviants—the group first pressures them to conform and, if they refuse, it rejects them (Schachter, 1951). Similar conformity pressures are at work in scientific communities; the community rejects and ostracizes scientists whose theories contradict the currently established notions (Campbell, 1969, p. 14). This happened to a geologist named Wegener who put forth the notion of "continental drift" (Ziman, 1968). He noticed that the coast lines of Africa and South America fit together like two puzzle pieces, and that the plants and animals living on the two

separate continents were remarkably alike. On the basis of these observations, he reasoned that the two continents had once been part of a
continuous land mass, which had split and gradually drifted apart (a
process still going on at the rate of approximately two centimeters per
year). Wegener's ideas were refuted by an esteemed Cambridge mathe-
matician who argued, through seismological evidence, that the earth was
too rigid to have undergone such disruptions of its surface, and for
fifty years continental drift remained a heresy. It was not until after
Wegener's death that his views were accepted.

It is in general wise for groups to discount single instances of non-
conformity or contradictoriness for, if astronomers chased after every
new star someone thought he saw, they would go on many a wild goose
chase (cf. Polanyi, 1969). It is also wise, however, for innovators like
Wegener to remain loyal to their own theories and perceptions, for they
may succeed in persuading an initially reluctant science to take them
seriously.

There have certainly been other Wegeners who have either not stuck
to their theories or not stayed in the field. Each reader may have his own
example—perhaps a teacher who resigned or whose contract was not
renewed because he was not doing acceptable research. It was not
"scholarly," his opposition said; it was too "radical," he replied.

Is there a place in scientific research for people with radically different visions? And if these people are not in the field now, is it possible
to recruit and train researchers from other groups, other classes, or
other persuasions without their losing, in the process, their original
social perspectives?

Implications for Society

The problems we have raised are not just problems for the ivory
tower. The errors, biases, values (and truths) to which social scientists
are heir have consequences outside their laboratories. Consider the rash
of studies done by the presidential commissions and government depart-
ments on violence, on the police, on the Kent State killings, on the black
family, and on the effects of television (National Advisory Commission
on Civil Disorders, 1968; National Commission on the Causes and Prevention of Violence, 1969; President's Commission on Campus Unrest,
1970; U.S. Department of Labor, 1965; and U.S. Public Health Service,

1972) and there are others to come. These studies are often done by social scientists who consciously or unconsciously bring their own values and perspectives to their work. And that work becomes the basis for broad social policy. As we come closer to a set of national social indicators measuring welfare or happiness (Land, 1971; U.S. Department of Health, Education & Welfare, 1969), and as we come closer to an experimenting society (e.g., Headstart programs, Sesame Street, negative income-tax experiments), it becomes crucial to protect our methods, our bookkeeping, and our interpretive skills from corruption and abuse.

The safeguards which we currently have are of two types. (1) There are internal rules of science which keep a scientist honest *within* the limitations of his questions, values, and perspectives. These include recording data systematically, reporting data fully, not ignoring disconfirming cases, abiding by the rules of statistical inference, controlling other sources of systematic or random variation, and letting the evidence fall where it may regardless of his or her desires. (2) There are the external arrangements described on page 15. We had eight categories of interviewers approach as many categories of interviewees to control for the inevitable biases of the backgrounds and perspectives of investigators. Campbell (1964) advocates an analogue to our design. He recommends at least a dual perspective on all intergroup research, with the added principle of reciprocity that "if I study you, you also study me." The following 2X2 table illustrates the arrangement:

Table 1-4

| | | Cultures or Groups Being Studied | |
		America	India
Persons doing the studying	Americans	A	B
	Indians	C	D

The predominant tendency to date has probably been for cultures to study themselves (cells A and D), and when crossgroup studies have been done, they have been unbalanced (with cell B fuller than C).

Researchers speaking on behalf of underrepresented groups (e.g., Greenglass & Stewart, 1973; see also Chapter 3 of this book) have begun to document this state of affairs: Greenglass and Stewart, sampling five well-known journals over a ten-year publication span, found that males were used as subjects five times as often as females in psychological studies; further, results from males-only studies tended strongly to be generalized, explicitly or implicitly, to "people at large," although the opposite was not true: when only females were used, conclusions were less frequently extended to other groups (see also Broverman et al., 1972). In a similar literature review, Prescott and Foster (1972) wrote and asked the investigators in some seventy studies published in a well-known journal in 1971 (1) why they had used only single-sex subjects in their work and (2) why they had chosen the sex they had (usually male). The extremely high rate of response from these investigators—over 85 percent—may be taken as an indication of the growing seriousness with which such questions of bias are being considered. The reasons most frequently given for single-sex investigations were: (1) the first or "basic" study in the area of psychology being investigated had been done on males, and further studies wanted comparability of results; (2) the research was done using students at a noncoed institution (usually male); and (3) since the investigators and their graduate-student assistants were more frequently of one sex than the other (again usually male), the use of same-sex subjects would avoid the complications of cross-sex interaction. All of these are understandable, pragmatic reasons which reflect the realistic limitations of institutional research—but one can easily see how they simply compound the problem with the passage of time. But, more optimistically, as prestigious research institutions continue to diversify their student bodies, as more marginal-group members become co-investigators, and as each of these groups develops its own theories and basic studies (e.g., Bardwick, 1972; Clark, 1973), we will have what amounts to more equal representation in all the cells of Table 1-4. If we go further and expose the data we gather and the theories we formulate from such studies to a wide range of critics, we also increase our chance of beating the problem of bias.

To every critic who charges us with being biased, we might extend an invitation to join in the cooperative venture. The more usual strategy is for investigators to study those groups which interest them personally and for later reviewers of the research to identify gaps in the field. In this way bias may be reduced in the long, if not the short, haul.
for it.

Chapter 2

Comparisons among Groups: Perceived Group Differences and Ethnocentrism

PROPOSITION

Interpersonal and intergroup similarity promote attraction, while dissimilarity is often a ground for dislike or outright disdain. Cultural and attitudinal similarity are more important than physical or racial similarity, although in the absence of explicit information about another's beliefs or cultural values, a stranger who differs racially is often assumed to differ in other ways too. In addition to such assumed differences, there are some real group differences which place considerable social distance between groups.

Illustrative Work

Interpersonal Similarity and Attraction Do we like people because they are like us? Or is the process an opposite one—that we *assume* people whom we like *are* like us? Or is it a little of both? Studies have indicated that, indeed, both things can happen—but the greater part of such research has focused on the first proposition, that when we compare ourselves with others and find similarities, we then tend to be attracted to those others.

Byrne (1969) and his coworkers have used a basic experimental procedure which has repeatedly shown that perceived similarity leads to interpersonal attraction. Students who have filled in an attitude questionnaire (usually in an earlier classroom session) are later asked to examine a similar questionnaire filled in by a "stranger." They then give their impressions of this stranger by filling out an Interpersonal Judgment Scale designed to elicit the degree of the student's liking for the stranger. In actuality the stranger is a fictitious person whose responses have been programmed to resemble those of the student to a greater or lesser degree. Using this procedure, Byrne and his colleagues have consistently found that the more the stranger is made to resemble the student, the greater degree of liking the student expresses for him. They have further shown that this relationship holds up among a great many other kinds of people besides students (something which, as we pointed out in Chapter 1, social science does not always demonstrate!).

In another pertinent experiment, Senn (1971) had pairs of male undergraduates perform a task together, and manipulated the feedback they got regarding how well they had done. He found that attraction to the other pair member was greatest when both members were told they had performed well, less when they were told they had both performed poorly, and least when they were told that one had done well and the other poorly. Not surprisingly, mutual attraction was greater when there was *positive* similarity ("We are alike; we both did well") than when there was *negative* similarity ("We are alike; we both did poorly"). When one member did well and the other did poorly, one might intuitively predict that there would be differential attraction, but in fact this was not the case; the degree of attraction was pretty much mutual, affirming again that it was degree of similarity that determined attraction— not degree of individual success at the task.

Race Versus Belief Similarity The positive relationship between similarity and attraction alone does not enable us to predict what any one person or group of persons thinks of another, even if we knew their real similarities and differences, for we must go on to ask, *Which* are the differences that matter? "People may be similar or different on any conceivable dimension upon which humans can be placed, and it seems quite unlikely that similarities such as length of big toe or social security number lead to attraction" (Berscheid & Walster, 1969, p. 69). Why, then, does racial similarity appear to be so salient in America at least?

Numerous studies have been conducted to determine whether physical similarity (such as race) is more or less important than philosophical similarity (such as belief in God) in determining interpersonal attraction. We shall describe the studies and their results because this is an important question and the data are intriguing. We shall also go on to suggest that it is a question which is difficult to answer, for some philosophical and methodological reasons which we shall explore.

The social psychologist Milton Rokeach and his colleagues have performed many experiments in which they present people with descriptions of a hypothetical "stimulus person" which include information about that person's race, occupation, belief in God, or personal philosophy. They have consistently found that people are more attracted to the person whose beliefs resemble their own rather than someone whose skin color or racial identification matches their own (e.g., Rokeach, 1961; Rokeach & Mezei, 1966; Rokeach & Parker, 1970; Rokeach et al., 1960). This interpretation suggests that in the absence of information about others' beliefs, Americans may mistakenly assume that persons of a different race hold different beliefs.

There is some evidence to suggest that this is what happens. In one study (Stein et al., 1965) ninth-grade students from white working-class homes were asked to react to six hypothetical teenagers whose descriptions fit the cells shown in the table on page 24.

The results showed that sharing the same beliefs was more important to these ninth-graders than being of the same race—they preferred teenagers A and B to teenagers C and D. When, however, the beliefs of the other person were *unknown,* these white respondents showed a preference for the teenager whose *race* was similar to their own; they preferred teenager E over person F (Stein et al., 1965). We may want to conclude that there is a purely *racist* element in human behavior whereby people feel attracted or hostile toward others solely on the basis of race. On the other hand, if we are convinced that *belief* similarity is the determining factor in intergroup or interpersonal attraction, then we might want to conclude that the white ninth-grade students were still operating on the basis of a presumed belief similarity, and that they

Table 2-1

| | | Race | |
		Same	Different
Beliefs	Same	A White teenager with beliefs similar to subject's	B Black teenager with beliefs similar to subject's
	Different	C White teenager with beliefs unlike the subject's	D Black teenager with beliefs unlike the subject's
	Unknown	E White teenager, beliefs unknown	F Black teenager, beliefs unknown

assumed that a white teenager's beliefs would be more similar to theirs than a black teenager's would.

The assumption that persons of a different race or ethnicity hold beliefs unlike one's own is a realistic assumption for certain kinds of beliefs. White and black persons in the United States have been found to differ in their beliefs about the causes and prevention of race riots and the reasons for economic inequalities. They differ, for instance, in the extent to which they believe that racial discrimination is to blame for the economic gap between blacks and whites: 70 percent of the black and only 56 percent of the white respondents felt that "Negroes miss out on jobs because of discrimination" (Campbell & Schuman, 1969).

This finding of real belief differences may help to explain why another social psychologist, Harry Triandis, and his colleagues have repeatedly found that for some persons in some situations, *racial* dissimilarity determines attraction. This is particularly true for intimate social relations (e.g., Triandis, 1961; Triandis & Davis, 1965; Byrne & Wong, 1962; Goldstein & Davis, 1972). Perhaps those persons who select their friends on the basis of racial similarity think that they are more likely to find congenial beliefs and values among them.

As important as the debate over the relative salience of belief versus race similarity is, let us examine why this may be an unresolvable issue. Suppose we wanted to determine which meant more to a child—receiving candy or avoiding a spanking. To test this we presented him with a choice between receiving two gumdrops or avoiding ten wallops on his bottom. We discovered that he would rather avoid the wallops and forgo his candy than vice versa, and concluded that physical punishments are more powerful than rewards. A critic might come along, however, and point out that we compared ten units of physical punishment with only two of reward, prompting us to repeat the study, this time offering the choice of two gumdrops or the avoidance of two wallops. No matter which the child chooses this time, a critic could again ask whether we had first established the equivalence of our units of physical punishment or reward. Perhaps the wallops were so hefty and the gumdrops so small that two of one were in no way objectively equivalent to two of the other. What we must do, therefore, is *scale* each of our dimensions, to establish how many wallops of a certain strength equal how many gumdrops of a certain size. Only then does it make sense for us to compare apples and oranges, as it were.

The same holds true for trying to assess the relative importance of race and belief similarity. We could, for instance, pit an inconsequential belief (such as how often one should brush one's teeth each day) against a more consequential race difference (such as Swedes versus Pygmies, who differ in physiognomy, skin color, and stature) only to find, lo and behold, that racial similarity is a more powerful determinant of attraction. Or we could pit a more consequential belief difference (such as whether or not one should sacrifice one's first-born child to the gods) against an undetectable race difference (such as a fair-skinned "black" and a swarthy "white") and find that belief similarity is what matters. These are of course extremely unbalanced cases and are not intended as criticisms of the research which we have cited on race versus belief similarity. Both Rokeach and Triandis used important beliefs (e.g., philosophical and religious values) and an important race distinction for Americans, at least (black versus white). We do want to point out, however, that no scaling efforts have been made that would equate the units of belief and race similarity, as we saw would have been necessary in the earlier illustration of candies and spankings. And perhaps no such scaling could ever be accomplished since the concept of race and race differences or similarities is even more elusive than are philosophical and religious beliefs. If anthropologists doubt the very validity of the concept of race, it hardly seems wise or worthwhile to attempt to scale the dimension.

We may, therefore, have to settle for the ambiguities left to us by past research. Some kinds of racial differences are important to some people in some situations; and beliefs matter more to other people under other circumstances. What is of interest to us, then, is discovering more about both the circumstances and the personal predispositions that interact to determine the relative importance of these two dimensions.

Social and Cultural Differences: Grounds for Ethnocentrism We have focused on racial differences and their attendant belief differences because these are the ones which preoccupy us in present-day America. When we speak of group differences, however, we include a host of other kinds of differences. (In fact, we would classify most racial differences as "imagined" rather than "real" in some absolute sense.) There are real differences, for instance between partilineal and matrilineal social organizations—in the former, the lines of inheritance and family name are passed on from father to son and, in the latter, from mother to daughter. There are real differences in cultural practices between those groups that eat pork and those that consider it unclean, between those who eat beef and those who consider it blasphemous, between those cultures that practice circumcision and those that do not. At the risk of opening a Pandora's box, we shall suggest that there are even agreed upon group differences in "national character." For instance, the Hidatsa Indians in the Dakotas and the local "pale-faced" ranchers agreed about the level of exchange of money and goods that each engaged in, and they agreed that they were different. But what they disagreed on were the evaluative labels which they attached to their own and the other's qualities. The table on page 27 illustrates their agreement on the factual differences and their disagreement about how good or bad each other's characteristics or traits were (Bruner, 1956).

The effect of these real group differences on intergroup attraction and hostility has been demonstrated by several social psychologists and anthropologists. An extensive survey of thirty tribes in East Africa asked fifty respondents in each tribe to indicate whether they would be willing to work, visit, eat with, or marry a person from each of thirteen other groups. In addition, the respondents were asked to indicate "which tribe is most similar to your own tribe" and "which tribe is least similar to your own tribe." Each tribe was then given a net simi-

Table 2-2

| | | Descriptions of | |
		Hidatsa	Ranchers
Descriptions by	Hidatsa	(Good) Generous, unselfish, share good fortune immediately with relatives and friends	(Bad) Stingy, selfish hoarders
	Ranchers	(Bad) Spendthrifty, improvident	(Good) Thrifty, provident

Source: Campbell, Donald T. *"Stereotypes and the Perception of Group Differences,"* American Psychologist 1967, p. 822.

larity score in relation to each other tribe by subtracting the number of times it was mentioned as least similar from the number of times it was named as most similar. The relationship between willingness to engage in social interaction and perceived similarity is positive and direct—the more similar the other tribe, the more willing persons were to work, visit, eat with and marry members from that group (Brewer, 1968; Campbell & LeVine, 1972). Tribes which share the same form of social organization (matrilineal versus patrilineal), the same linguistic origins, or a belief in a common ancestor are also more kindly disposed toward one another.

The research we have described gives us some clues as to which differences matter in how groups react to one another. But, is there perhaps some rule or logic that governs the selection of differences? Surely we could think of many ways in which any two groups differ, yet some differences are ignored while others are focused upon. One social psychologist who has looked for the logic behind intergroup relations suggests that "the greatest contrasts provide the strongest stimuli," and so he proposes the following:

The greater the real differences between groups on any particular custom, detail of physical appearance, or item of material culture, the more likely it is that that feature will appear in the stereotyped imagery each group has of the other. (Campbell, 1967, p. 821)

He goes on to suggest that if a group ostracizes or punishes its own members for their differences on some trait or dimension, then that same trait will be used as a yardstick for measuring the acceptability of out-groups:

> . . . if an out-group shows a behavior for which in-group members are regularly punished or despised, this behavior is much more apt to be noticed and made a part of the out-group stereotype than some other trait for which responses are less ingrained. Thus . . . the Gusii ridicule uncircumcised children for their childishness and accuse an older boy still uncircumcised of cowardice. This provides a familiar stimulus-response bias for out-group stereotypes about their uncircumcising Luo neighbors. Similarly, the Gusii child-rearing emphasis on modesty regarding nudity and elimination provides a familiar association base for stereotypes of both Luo and Kipsigis, since both differ from the Gusii in these customs (Campbell, 1967, pp. 822-823).

From these studies it can be seen that the study of which group differences matter is very much in its infancy and very rich in research potential.

Ethnocentrism as a Means of Enhancing In-group Solidarity It should be borne in mind that as a group focuses on the *larger* differences between itself and an out-group, the relatively *smaller* in-group differences start to seem inconsequential. In other words, comparison and conflict with a third party, or out-group, often heightens mutual attraction and solidarity among the in-group. This is a proposition which has been repeatedly suggested and demonstrated by social scientists. Georg Simmel stated that "a certain amount of . . . outer controversy is organically tied up with the very elements that ultimately hold the group together" (1955, p. 17). Lewis Coser elaborating on Simmel's ideas, suggested that "If the basic social structure is stable, if basic values are not questioned, cohesion is usually strengthened by war through challenge to, and revitalization of, values and goals which have been taken for granted" (1956, p. 90).

It has always seemed, at first glance, paradoxical that during times of war, the mental health of the civilian population seems to get better, not worse. During World War II, British hospitals braced themselves for a huge rise in the incidence of emotional disturbance as a result of the life-disrupting, unpredictable air raids. But the rate of hospital admissions, in fact, went down, and did not begin to rise again until after the end of the war. Similar data from Norway, France, Belgium, and the

United Kingdom showed much the same pattern—"either a reduction or no significant increase in admission rates, particularly for psychoses" (Arthur, 1971, p. 90). In a similar vein, the French sociologist Emile Durkheim, in his landmark work on the correlates of suicide, has demonstrated that great political upheavals that involve people at a grass-roots level are regularly accompanied by a *decrease* in the rate of suicide, a trend that cannot be accounted for merely by poorer recordkeeping procedures. He concludes that

> . . . these facts are therefore susceptible of only one interpretation; namely, that great social disturbances and popular wars rouse collective sentiments, stimulate partisan spirit and patriotism . . . and, concentrating activity toward a single end, at least temporarily cause a stronger integration of society . . . . As [the struggles] force men to close ranks and confront a common danger, the individual thinks less of himself and more of the common cause (Durkheim, 1951, pp. 203–208).

Right up to the present, the evidence accumulates that conflict enhances cohesiveness and lowers the rate of emotional disturbance and antisocial behavior within groups. Solomon et al. (1965), using official crime reports, medical records, and newspaper accounts of three black, Southern communities, found that there was a substantial decrease in crimes of violence during "periods of organized protests and 'direct action' for civil rights" during the early sixties. These statistical trends were confirmed by interviews with residents of these towns. One student pointed out that during such periods of activism, "a cat would have something to live for—not just a five-day week, then get it off his chest by getting drunk on Saturday night," and another local black leader asserted that "by 1963, there was a unification of common interest, and people who before were indigent and depressed suddenly found that they had something to live and fight for." Again, in the early 1970s, with the resurgence of conflict in Northern Ireland, there has been a decline in the rate of both suicides and mental hospital admissions (CBC, 1972). And although systematic research has yet to be reported on the results of joining causes such as the women's movement, gay liberation, or red power, anecdotal evidence points to a similar conclusion: that direct action against a commonly perceived opponent is one way in which movement solidarity is achieved. We will develop this and other themes regarding liberation movements more fully in Chapter 5.

There also exists *experimental* evidence for the integrative effects of comparison and conflict with outsiders. Perhaps the most ambitious demonstration of this took place in the early fifties when Sherif (1961) turned an entire summer-camp operation into an exercise in conflict and cooperation. In one phase of this study, two carefully matched groups of boys were brought together in a whole series of planned encounters, such as baseball games, tugs-of-war, treasure hunts, and other contests, with the ultimate result that neither group wanted to have anything to do with the other. This was confirmed by asking members of each group to rate their friends, and the resultant *sociometric index* showed that over 90 percent of the members of each group chose members of their own group as friends. It would seem that a definite "we-they" or "good-guys-bad-guys" polarization had taken place, with each side convinced, of course, that they themselves were the "good guys."

These "quasi-therapeutic" effects of conflict—that is, the heightening of morale, satisfaction, and in-group solidarity as a result of conflict with outsiders—have also been suggested in a more recent laboratory experiment. Aronson and Cope (1968) arranged for students taking a "test" of creativity to get either harsh or pleasant feedback from the experimenter. Subsequently they heard this same experimenter (a graduate student) receive either praise or abuse from his supervisor regarding an issue totally different from the experiment itself. The question Aronson and Cope were asking was: "Is my enemy's enemy my friend?" In other words, would the students feel more kinship, or solidarity, with the supervisor who abused the experimenter who had abused them? The postexperimental ratings of the supervisor's attractiveness by the students showed that this was indeed the case; the maligned student and the supervisor were alike in their "dislike" of the experimenter, hence the student's enhanced feelings of liking for the supervisor himself.

Some Explanations of Ethnocentrism

Similarity Affects Self-esteem We spoke earlier about the extent to which differences perceived as important lead to hostility and contempt between persons and groups. Why should dissimilarity lead to dislike, especially when common wisdom has it not only that birds of a feather flock together but indeed that opposites attract? One hint comes from a study by Walster and Walster (1963) who showed that if students were assured of being *liked* beforehand, they tended to choose *dissimilar* others as friends, but when not so assured, they chose *similar* others. This suggests that our tendency to prefer similar others may often mere-ly reflect our need to be liked and our assumption that we are more *likely* to be liked by those whom we resemble. Just as black and white teenagers assumed that superficial racial similarity was an index of deeper belief similarity unless they knew otherwise, we may also assume that those who most resemble us—whether superficially or deeply—will like us most, unless we have additional information to the contrary.

Conversely, we often automatically assume that those who seem very different from us must be disdainful of us, and of our particular abilities, so we reciprocate with a dislike that may partly mask a sense of our own inferiority or low self-esteem. We will now examine a num-ber of studies that suggest that the degree to which we value ourselves and our own abilities can depend in part on the degree to which we interact with people whose abilities seem similar or dissimilar to our own.

One of the most dramatic demonstrations of dependence on others to determine self-esteem and self-confidence was done by Davis (1966), who collected data on occupational aspirations from 35,000 male college students receiving their bachelor's degree in 1961. He found, not sur-prisingly, that there was a strong positive relationship between the stu-dents' grades and the quality of their college on the one hand, and scholastic-aptitude test-scores on the other. But a more surprising find-ing was that students' level of occupational aspiration (that is, the de-gree to which they sought a prestigious, "high academic-performance career field") was less related to their school's prestige than to the stu-dents' grades within the school. In other words, the students' *relative standing* among their peers at their own school was the main factor that predicted whether they felt "good enough" to become a doctor, lawyer, scientist, or university professor. The importance of relative grade standing persists in Davis' data despite a tremendous variety in quality of schools, and even in spite of differences in reported ease of getting good grades. Davis rather aptly entitled this study "The Campus as Frogpond," reflecting the truism that a big frog in a small pond will aim his sights higher than an equally talented frog stuck in a larger pond.

Other studies also bear out this notion that our own self esteem is influenced by our perceptions of other people's worth. Morse and Gergen (1970) ran a naturalistic experiment in which participants thought they were actually responding to an ad for a job as a research assistant in a psychology department. As each of the "applicants" filled out a number of personality-assessment forms said to be relevant to the selection procedure, a second "applicant" (actually an experimental confederate) was brought into the same room and told to complete the same forms. In half the cases, this stooge applicant gave an impression of neatness, efficiency, and competence, complete with such props as dark suit, attaché case, slide rule, and a high level statistics book in hand ("Mr. Clean"). In the remaining instances, the stooge-applicant was dirty and disheveled (even by the casual dress standards of today's colleges) and bumbled his way through the forms in an apparently helpless and incompetent manner ("Mr. Dirty"). Over and above this contrast, half the Mr. Cleans and half the Mr. Dirtys were said to be applying for the *same* job as the naive applicant, while the other half were said to be applying for a totally different one.

The procedure was so planned that, among other things, the naive applicant had to fill out two different scales assessing degree of self-esteem. One of these he had completed before Mr. Clean or Mr. Dirty joined him. He did not fill out the other (near the end of his stack of forms) until after the stooge applicant had been in the room with him for several minutes. What Morse and Gergen expected was the possibility that the applicant's self-esteem would change as a result of exposure to the stooge applicant. They hypothesized that self-esteem would go up among applicants comparing themselves to bumbling Mr. Dirty, and down among applicants exposed to competent Mr. Clean. This turned out to be the case: "The socially desirable stimulus person produced a significant decrease in self-esteem while the undesirable other significantly enhanced subjects' self-estimates" (Morse & Gergen, p. 148). In fact, so strong was the impact of the mere appearance of Mr. Clean and Mr. Dirty that it totally wiped out the difference predicted to occur between "competing" and "non-competing" conditions. One would have thought that the obtained changes in self-esteem would be greater among those applicants who thought the stooge was competing for the same job as they—a situation with high *utility of comparison* (Jones & Gerard, 1967), but this did not turn out to be the case. This supports a contention of Singer (1966), who maintains that people do not evaluate just a single opinion or ability at a time but rather compare their *whole selves* to others to arrive at a generalized feeling of self-esteem.

One other, although less strong, finding in the Morse and Gergen study bears mention: if applicants rated themselves as similar to the stooge (regardless of whether it was Mr. Clean or Mr. Dirty) their self-esteem tended to go up; if they rated themselves as dissimilar, their measured self-esteem tended to go down. So it seems that people not only *choose* similar others as standards for comparison but also derive a feeling of self-validation from more similar others. "When another is seen as similar to self, he places a stamp of legitimacy on one's conduct or appearance . . . [whereas] encountering an individual whose characteristics differ from one's own may initiate a process of self-questioning and doubt" (p. 154).

We began this section by examining a study in which the self-esteem of white college students was shown to alter with the nature of groups to which they compared themselves. We will conclude with a pair of studies—one a laboratory study, the other based on school records—which demonstrate a similar process taking place in black students.

Katz et al. (1964) had a sample of male students from a predominantly black college in the South and another sample from a nearby predominantly white college perform a "digit-symbol" task. This simply required the students to match sets of geometric symbols to numbers according to a standard code given at the top of the page. At each college, participants were divided into three groups. One group was told that the test was strictly local and would be used to evaluate and advise students in comparison with their fellow students at that college. A second group was told that the test was being run nationally, and that their scores would be compared to those of students at almost every other American university. The third group was not told anything about a comparison group. In this experiment, it was not the students' self-esteem or level of aspiration that was being measured, but their actual performance on the task. The results indicated that the black college students as a group did better when they believed their scores would be compared to local (black college) norms than when they believed their scores would be compared to national norms (which would be derived mostly from the scores of white students). By contrast, no such difference appeared in the white sample. It is possible that this difference in performance among the black students reflected corresponding fluctuations in anxiety and self-esteem as they anticipated being compared with either an all-black norm or an essentially all-white one. This possibility recalls the criticism of "white" IQ tests mentioned in Chapter 1.

More recently, Weber et al. (1971) looked at records on achievement-test scores and academic "self-concept" (self-esteem) scores collected from samples of black and white children both before and after the formal integration of a school system in the Midwest. The achievement-test scores, collected by a national agency known as Educational Testing Service, were to assess how well the students were actually doing academically. The academic self-concept (ASC) scores were obtained from answers to such questions as, How well did you do in school this year? How hard did you work? How well could you do if you really worked at it? How would you say your schoolwork compares with the schoolwork of the other students in your class? These ASC scores were assumed to reflect how "good" the students felt about their ability and performance in school. It was found that even though their actual achievement scores went *up,* the academic self-concept scores of black children went *down* after school integration. Among white students, not only did achievement scores stay rather stable from before to after integration, but self-concept scores stayed much more so, relative to those of the black students. Although the nature of this study was such that interpretations must be made with caution, it again suggests that when people have to start playing in a league many of whose members they perceive as having a different level of skill, their estimates of their own self-worth change accordingly.

Similarity Is Positively Reinforcing Some ingenious experiments have been designed to demonstrate that attitude statements that are similar to a person's own beliefs serve as positive reinforcers. Subjects in these studies were trained on simple discrimination-learning tasks in which they had to learn to choose the correct stimulus from pairs differing in shape (square versus circle), color (green versus red), and size (large versus small). After each choice they were either reinforced by receiving a card with an attitude statement or not reinforced (by receiving a blank card). In one experiment the subjects had to learn always to choose the square rather than the circle, no matter what the color or shape, and they learned this much more quickly when they were reinforced with attitude statements that were *similar* to their own positions (Kian et al., 1973). This finding has been obtained repeatedly (e.g., Golightly & Byrne, 1964), indicating that attitudinal similarity is a positive reinforcer just as food, water, or nods of the head are.

We might chalk this phenomenon up to man's inherent narcissism, or we might take a more sympathetic look at what the reinforcing effect of attitudinal and interpersonal similarity in general means. It seems not implausible that attitudinal and other forms of similarity provide consensual validation which is needed as much by men on the street as by scientists in their labs. Finding someone else whose attitudes, beliefs, cultural practices, or taboos coincide with one's own provides confirmation of one's ways. Unlike the physical world where our beliefs about the length of lines or shape of objects can be validated by physical yardsticks, the social world provides no uniform system of weights or measures against which to check our beliefs. Our only source of validation is other persons, and each like-minded person provides an additional datum that we are correct (cf. Festinger, 1950, 1954a, 1954b). In the social as well as the martial arena, therefore, we acquire a sense of strength in numbers.

Unanswered Questions

At one point in this chapter it was suggested that in deciding which are the crucial differences between groups, a given group will focus on those differences whose appearance in their *own* group is considered deviant. Hence, because the Gusii consider lack of circumcision an index of childishness and cowardice within their own group, the norm of non-circumcision among their Luo neighbors becomes a difference that is particularly salient. But one might explain this perceived difference the opposite way around: not that in-group ideas of abnormality lead to the selective perception of out-group differences, but that the perception of differences leads to new concepts of deviance within the group. By this reasoning, the difference in circumcision practice between groups is what is noticed first, and only after that do the Gusii start saying to their uncircumcised males, "You are deviant because you are acting like a Luo." The selection of one explanation over the other is a little like asking which came first, the chicken or the egg, or in more social-scientific language, a question about *direction of causality*. It should be borne in mind that such questions cannot be answered unless we have a clear indication of the time sequence involved: did the Gusii contempt for noncircumcision precede or follow their first contact with their uncircumcised Luo neighbors? Such time sequences can be determined with relative ease in a controlled laboratory study, but are almost impossible to establish in a field study involving groups whose history of contact is long and complex. Hence it is important to realize that while intergroup differences and hostility may be clearly *documented*, the causal *explanations* often remain a matter of conjecture.

Another question we might ask is whether it is only competition against an out-group that promotes solidarity among in-group members. We have been focusing on the benefits of *conflict*—but could we not just as easily point to the benefits of *cooperation?* Could it be that cooperation among in-group members to attain a goal that benefits them all will enhance the attraction of in-group members towards each other, whether this goal involves the elimination of a perceived opponent or something entirely different?

Morton Deutsch (1949) has developed a theory of cooperation and competition postulating just such a relationship between cooperation and interpersonal attraction. He defines cooperation as a situation where individuals' joint efforts attain a mutually beneficial goal that none of them could attain (or attain as easily) alone, and suggests that such cooperation enhances interpersonal attraction. Competition, on the other hand, since it denies the desired goal to one of the contending parties, results in lessened interpersonal attraction.

Deutsch's theory maintains that it is the actual, pretask *motivation*, or intention to cooperate towards a common goal, that is at the root of enhanced interpersonal attraction among teammates. But other researchers (Zajonc & Marin, 1967) suggest that even in apparently cooperating groups it is the successful *results* of cooperation, not the act of cooperating per se, that enhance interpersonal attraction. We all know how a team can feel towards one of its members who, with the best intention of cooperating towards a win, keeps striking out. Zajonc and Marin demonstrated in a laboratory setting that attraction is greatest towards the person who "least retards" the individual's progress towards a goal, whether that person is a competent teammate or an incompetent opponent! They set up a game in which points were supposedly determined by quick reaction time, and in which pairs of players could get a prize only by pooling the points they gained against an opposing pair. In reality, the points won were programmed so that in each pair, one teammate won 80 percent of the total points, the other won only 20 percent, and their pooled total was just shy of the number of points needed to qualify for the $10 prize. Thus neither pair actually "won."

In a later assessment of attraction to both one's teammate and one's opponent, it was found that the "competent" players (those who got 80 percent of their side's points) liked their "incompetent" opponents (whose incompetence *facilitated* their own gain in points) better than their incompetent teammates (whose incompetence had *prevented* the team from actually winning the prize). For the incompetent players, the opposite relationship held: they preferred their competent teammates over their competent opponents (whose skill had prevented them personally from contributing to a win for their own team).

This study by Zajonc and Marin suggests that possibly conflict against out-groups facilitates in-group solidarity only if all members pull their weight equally well in the struggle, which is an affirmation of the similarity-attraction thesis in that "equally competent" teammates have very similar abilities. On the other hand, these findings also suggest a limitation to the similarity-attraction thesis, which would predict that competent players would feel equally unattracted to both the incompetent teammate and the incompetent opponent—who are both, after all, equally "unlike" the competent player—and likewise for the incompetent player. Instead they found that the basis for interpersonal attraction was evidently not *similarity of ability* (as in experiments described earlier) but rather the degree to which the other facilitated one's own goal attainment. Most experiments involving implicit comparison of task abilities are done in a context which involves neither explicit cooperation nor competition. Perhaps we need one statement about attraction as it is related to similarity of *personality* or *ability,* and another regarding similarity of *goals.* In studies that do not explicitly set a common goal to be reached through cooperation or competition, it appears that persons are attracted to those who have the same *ability.* But from the Zajonc and Marin study we reach a different conclusion: where an explicit goal is aimed for, attraction varies in proportion to the degree that the other is facilitating (as a teammate *or* an opponent) our own arrival at the desired goal; this places much more weight on *outcome* than on prior motivation, disposition, or ability.

Implications for Society

One implication for society from the studies cited in this chapter concerns the evidence that self-esteem—especially concerning one's own abilities—appears to be influenced by the degree of similarity between ourselves and those with whom we work or interact. This suggests that some people may *protect* their self-image by restricting their range of contacts with people dissimilar to themselves. While such a strategy might be *personally* beneficial, continued lack of contact with other groups could lead to progressively greater intergroup differences and a consequent escalation of hostility. How can we encourage the intergroup contact that would seem to be an essential prerequisite for harmonious relations without, at the same time, producing a contrast of certain skills and abilities which may lower the self-esteem and performance of the individuals of either group? If we return to the Morse and Gergen study in which students compared themselves to Mr. Clean or Mr. Dirty, we may find at least one answer to this question. In addition to the other measures, Morse and Gergen looked at self-esteem as a function of the subject's perceived *self-consistency.* This was a personality measure of the extent to which each subject felt his most important traits were compatible with each other—a measure, so to speak, of his feeling of being "together." It was found that self-consistent subjects had much more stable self-esteem scores than non-self-consistent subjects. Non-self-consistent subjects tended to be highly affected by either stooge: exposed to Mr. Clean, their self-esteem plummeted; exposed to Mr. Dirty, their self-esteem soared. In self-consistent subjects, these respective changes were much smaller. This suggests that while perceptions of others' worth do indeed contribute to fluctuations in our own self-esteem, there are still individual differences (such as self-consistency) that modify this effect. We leave it to the developmental and personality psychologists to suggest the conditions of upbringing which best ensure such "togetherness," merely noting here that internal as well as external factors influence our ability to face new social environments as positive learning experiences rather than as threats to our own self-esteem and that of our respective groups.

A second implication of social-comparison research as we have laid it out is the matter of manipulating solidarity through the engineering of intergroup conflict. In the Sherif study, where competing sets of campers showed higher in-group morale as a result of induced rivalry between the groups, there is what some might consider a very strong hint of social engineering. In a similar study (Julian et al., 1966), army squads forced to compete against each other showed higher morale and adjustment to army life than did their noncompeting fellows. The researchers of this study conclude:

> The importance of this experiment is probably in the demonstration that task groups under field conditions can be engineered by appropriate environmental manipulation to contribute to the individual group member's adjustment. It further shows that such effects can be accomplished through administrative channels within the context of routine operational conditions rather than through the intervention of mental health specialists. . . . In light of the critical shortage of professional personnel in the mental health field, the possibility of promoting better adjustment through relatively minor changes in the administrative structure opens an exciting vista of future possibilities (p. 326).

This "exciting vista of future possibilities" naturally presupposes the morality of the cause to which people are being so successfully "adjusted." Certainly there will be differential support in our own society for the idea of promoting satisfaction with an institution whose orientation seems to stress the elimination of out-group members much more often than the defense of lives within the in-group. Most of us are shocked when we see the Nazi propaganda films which depicted brutelike Jews and Poles assaulting innocent Aryan maidens—films developed with the goal of inflaming hostility against these groups and building up the militant nationalism necessary to proceed with their persecution. But is this qualitatively different from the promotion of labels like "slant-eyes," "gooks," and "slope-heads," with the result that one has managed to maximize perceived dissimilarity and hence the perceived justice of indiscriminate killing? Some will see a clear moral difference between the two situations; others will see them as one and the same thing— but the point to be emphasized here is that the discovery of lawful social-scientific relationships in no way guarantees the particular use to which they are put.

What, then, are the possible substitute bases for solidarity besides conflict and in-group–out-group comparisons? Is it possible to find William James' "moral equivalent of war"? There is certainly evidence to suggest that the existence of a common goal decreases intergroup hostility, and that this common goal need not be a third body of people against which both groups form an alliance. In the Sherif summer-camp study, even after the hostile polarization of the two groups of boys had taken place, the creation of common problems and tasks whose solution was clearly beneficial to both groups was enough to foster new friendships across group lines: as the two hostile groups were brought together to set up campsites, decide on movies to be seen, search out a fault in the water supply, or tow a truck several hundred yards to get it started, the quality of interaction between the groups became progressively friendlier until, at camp's end, there was a mutual decision to ride home together in the same bus. This change was confirmed by analogous changes in sociometric ratings, which now showed many more friendship choices across group lines.

A second study (Feshbach & Singer, 1957) showed that racial prejudice was greater among groups of students who were made to dwell on the possibility of *personal* crises (such as marital discord, mental breakdown, or accident) than among control groups. However, groups of students who discussed the possibility of *shared* crises, such as floods, hurricanes, or atomic war, showed less prejudice than the control groups. The feelings of whites towards blacks varied in this way despite the fact that neither type of crisis involved blacks as either a threat or source of support. This suggests that attitudes toward an out-group can deteriorate in the face of a variety of personal traumas among in-group members. Actual conflict with the out-group is not a necessary precondition. But, more optimistically, the study also suggests that a feeling of unity in crisis among the in-group may generalize to better feelings about an out-group. Perhaps reminders about the ultimate chanciness of life and property occasioned by disasters help to emphasize the common vulnerability of all people to such crises, and from this newly perceived similarity comes a wider intergroup attraction.

Chapter 3

Competition between Groups: Relative Deprivation and Dissatisfaction

PROPOSITION

We generally gauge our own satisfactions by comparing our lot with that of others. Even when not in face-to-face contact with others, we use their outcomes and relative positions as a yardstick for judging our own. The rules governing these comparison processes ensure that we usually compare ourselves with, and thus compete with, only similar others. Occasionally these bounds are broken, however, and we compare ourselves with persons whose status is either far above or below ours. When this happens, the gross discrepancies revealed are no longer tolerable, and riots or revolutions may result.

Illustrative Work

How Comparison Determines Satisfaction: In Which League Are You Playing? We are all familiar with the concept of athletic leagues and classes. There are major leagues, minor leagues, and little leagues in baseball; first and second divisions in soccer; light-, middle-, and heavy-weight classes in boxing and wrestling. It never occurs to us to judge the performance of a middleweight boxer against the accomplishments of a heavyweight like Muhammed Ali, or a major league pitcher's fast ball against that of the best little league player. The dimension of superior and inferior performance in any sport is not a continuous one for all participants, but is considered relative only to that category (age, weight, sex, or whatever) to which a given player is assigned.

There is evidence to suggest that people extend this "league" concept to judgments of their own satisfaction or dissatisfaction with a host of other, nonathletic situations. Runciman (1966) points out that after disasters such as earthquakes, floods, or tornadoes, certain people suffering moderately heavy damage are often less unhappy than others who have sustained only light damage. The reason, says Runciman, is that members of the first group were typically located near to, but not actually in the center of, the disaster zone, and, comparing themselves to the major victims, consider themselves lucky to have been spared the worst. But the second group, located near but not quite outside the area of destruction, typically compare themselves to those who escaped completely and therefore feel put upon. The degree of resignation or indignation would seem to depend on what "disaster league" the victims assigned themselves to.

Another famous set of studies (Stouffer et al., 1949; Merton & Kitt, 1950) uncovered some surprising findings about American soldiers' satisfaction with promotion during World War II. Promotions in the Air Corps were rapid and widespread, whereas among the Military Police they were slow and unpredictable. Intuitively, then, one would expect the Air Corpsmen to be more satisfied about their chances for promotion, since, as a group, they actually *were* moving ahead much faster than the MPs. In fact, the Air Corpsmen expressed considerable frustration over their rate of promotion, while the MPs showed greater contentment and higher morale generally. It seems that the Air Corpsmen's generous rate of promotion led them all to adopt very high levels of aspiration. The sky (if one can excuse the pun) was the limit, and anything short of that left them with a sense of having been cheated. By contrast, the MPs did not expect frequent promotions, and were thus content with what few gains they did make. Stouffer and his colleagues coined the term *relative deprivation*—the discrepancy between what one anticipates and what one attains—to describe the state of mind of the Air Corpsmen, whose low morale had less to do with their absolute level of attainment than with this feeling of being deprived relative to what they considered possible. The MPs, on the other hand, considered any promotion an unexpected benefit, and as a result experienced *relative gratification*.

It may be useful at this point to draw the distinction between *membership groups* and *reference groups* (Hyman, 1942). A membership group is a group to which a person actually belongs, but a reference group is that group which is employed as a standard for evaluation of a person's own position. People may use their own membership group as their reference group also—such is the case in the example just cited of the Air Corpsmen and the MPs. But they need not do so.

Another of Stouffer's World War II studies (Stouffer et al., 1949) compared the morale of enlistees who had a high school education with those who had none. He found the latter less satisfied with life in the army not because of their relative standing among enlistees but because of the deprivations compared with friends back home. During the war, persons who were working on farms or in heavy industry were given draft exemptions because their domestic production was necessary for a nation at war. These draft-exempt persons generally had less than a high school education, so those unlucky ones who *were* drafted from that educational level felt as though they had been singled out for dangerous duty. Like the victims at the edge of the earthquake, they were faced with the question: Why me?

More recently, research on race relations has also supported the notion that satisfaction or dissatisfaction with one's lot depends in some way on one's choice of reference groups (Ransford, 1968; Sears & McConahy, 1970). Moreover, the degree of relative deprivation appears to be a good predictor of activism directed towards *reducing* this gap between attainment and expectation. The Sears and McConahy study sample-surveyed the attitudes of Los Angeles ghetto residents soon after the Watts riot of August, 1965, in an attempt to assess the correlates of riot participation. They wondered just what differences (if any) regarding background, age, education, and attitudes distinguished those who had actually taken part in the Watts riots from those who had merely observed or stayed totally aloof. They found, first of all, that riot participants were more apt to be younger than nonparticipants and also more likely to be native to Los Angeles rather than recent migrants from the

South. But beyond these simple demographic indices, they found that the *region of socialization*–the area where one was raised (North or South)–was related to feelings of relative deprivation, and that feelings of relative deprivation, in turn, were related to riot participation.

More specifically, it has been a well-documented finding of the 1960s (Beardwood, 1968; Brink & Harris, 1966; Pettigrew, 1964) that Southern-raised blacks expressed less discontent than their Northern cousins with regard to a number of issues: housing, school integration, transportation, the police, treatment by white businessmen, etc. This would seem to be because Southern blacks, as well as others who have only recently left the South, have had fewer resources in their own past (since the South is generally less affluent than the North) and, in terms of intergroup relations, have had a much more restricted range of people with whom they compared their lot: historically, they might have been persuaded to make comparisons with other blacks. On the other hand, young Northern-raised blacks might be accustomed not only to a generally higher standard of living but also to a world which was less rigidly segregated and which therefore implicitly encouraged them (unlike their Southern cousins) to aspire to the same achievements as their white city-mates. Relative to both these yardsticks (general level of material affluence and general rate of social mobility), black Northerners would predictably feel more deprived than those from the South: The Southern-raised persons used only their own membership group as a reference group, while the Northerners were more apt to use whites as a reference group.

Sears and McConahy, in the Watts study, constructed a scale of relative deprivation by asking persons to state, first, what kind of work they were *then* doing, and, second, what kind of work they would most *like* to do if they had an unrestricted choice. The gap between the social-prestige level of the actual job and the desired job was assumed to be a measure of dissatisfaction or relative deprivation if the desired job was of higher prestige than the actual job, and satisfaction or relative gratification if the desired job was of the same or lower prestige than the actual job. By this measure, Los Angeles natives and migrants from other Northern areas, in line with prediction, scored much more deprived than migrants from the South–particularly among the young. In addition, significantly more of the former had been active in the Watts riot, a point to which we will return in Chapter 5.

Another way of conceptualizing the above findings is in terms of Thibaut and Kelley's (1959) notions of *comparison level* (CL) and *comparison level for alternatives* (CLalt). The CL is a type of average value of all of a person's known, relevant outcomes regarding a given issue, those experienced vicariously as well as those experienced directly. If you can imagine a seesaw with satisfying outcomes ranged along one side of the balance and shading into unsatisfying outcomes on the other side, the CL would be the neutral point between the two categories, and against which any outcome would be gauged as relatively satisfying or dissatisfying. The location of the CL is said to depend a great deal on the *range* of one's past, experienced outcomes—both good and bad. By this standard, Northern blacks, living in a generally more prosperous society and hence having experienced a wider range of "good" outcomes, would be expected to have a different CL than Southern blacks of more restricted experience. Relating this to the vocabulary we have used previously in this chapter, the relatively gratified Southern-raised migrants were experiencing outcomes at or above their CL, while the relatively deprived Northern-raised residents were experiencing outcomes *below* their CL.

The *comparison level for alternatives* (CLalt) is the CL adjusted for *perceived availability* of alternative outcomes. Whereas the CL is the neutral point between satisfaction and dissatisfaction, the CLalt is the neutral point between acceptance and rejection. This is an interesting additional concept because it points up that a situation may be *unsatisfying* according to one's CL, yet *acceptable* according to one's CLalt (as when one accepts the lesser of two evils or the best of a bad deal). Similarly, a situation can be satisfying according to one's CL, yet unacceptable according to one's CLalt. (After all, why choose hamburger when you're being offered *roast beef?)* It is quite possible that many black Southerners living in Northern urban areas had at least been exposed to as rich and complex an environment as their Northern urban neighbors—and hence had similar CLs for gauging satisfaction or dissatisfaction with their lot. But in the 1960s the black Southern city dwellers may have perceived many of these outcomes as available only to whites (since few if any blacks could be observed enjoying them), whereas the Northerners, exposed to a greater *integration of outcomes,* would come to assume that such outcomes were accessible to them also. While the CLs of the two groups might be the same, the CLalts would be very different. Again, to integrate this concept with previous ones: the Northerners' different CLalt could be related to their having adopted a reference group (Northern white society in general) different from that of Southern blacks, for evaluating their own satisfaction, while few if any of the Southerners would use as a reference group anyone outside their own membership group.

An Alternative Interpretation of Relative Deprivation Much of the early work on relative deprivation appeared paradoxical—precisely those who objectively were best off appeared to be most dissatisfied. It was as though they were ungrateful wretches who, when you gave them an inch, wanted to take a mile. The argument which we shall develop here does not dispute the fact that selective comparisons are made, but it does question the meaning which has often been attached to the process.

Recently, several social psychologists have questioned the early interpretation of relative deprivation and have argued that dissatisfaction is not a result of imagined or exaggerated deprivations but rather of real inequalities. Sawyer (1971) contrasts three ways people may operate when faced with the problem of a limited supply and a large demand for commodities (be these grades, incomes, television sets, or whatever else we covet). A person may opt to *maximize* his or her own rewards, paying no attention to what others receive; Sawyer calls this an *individualistic* orientation. One may try to maximize one's own rewards *relative* to others' rewards; this he calls a *competitive* orientation. Or one may try to maximize equality by *minimizing* the differences between oneself and others, regardless of who may have the advantage; this is a *cooperative* orientation. Symbolic representations of these three orientations appear in Figure 3-1.

If M is My achievement and O is the Other person's achievement:
- (a) Individualism = Maximize M
- (b) Competition (relative deprivation) = Maximize M–O or Minimize O–M
- (c) Cooperation (Equality) = Minimize $|M-O|$, the absolute difference between M and O

Figure 3-1 Three approaches to the distribution of rewards. (*Adapted from Sawyer, 1966.*)

Sawyer notes that the flavor of much of the older literature on relative deprivation carries with it the implication that the cause of discontent lies in people's competitive nature—that they want to outstrip their neighbors or their particular set of Joneses. A more generous interpretation may be that these persons have a cooperative orientation and are trying not to outdo someone else but rather to maximize equality and minimize all differences, regardless of who may be on top.

Sawyer has some data which show that college students prefer to maximize *equality* and give everyone Bs rather than compete for grades and see some people receive Cs while others walk off with As (Sawyer, 1966). Nine- and ten-year old boys also worked to maximize equality while playing a game in which the payoffs were quarters and dollars (Morgan & Sawyer, 1967). It would appear that those studies which have examined the feelings of satisfaction of persons who are receiving less than others may have a difficult time distinguishing between a desire to minimize O-M and a desire to achieve equality by minimizing all absolute differences or | M-O |. And yet it is important that the latter not be ignored as a possible interpretation, for "feeling deprived and covetous because another person has more is very different from desiring a society where the quality of life is equally good for all" (Sawyer, 1971, p. 98).

Sawyer's work thus leads us to focus on the objective and not merely the subjective deprivations, and the *real* and not simply the perceived inequalities between groups.

Blocked Opportunity Theory of Conflict and Conflagration After the Watts, Detroit, and Newark riots in the 1960s, social scientists began to turn their attention away from an almost exclusive concern with the attitudes of white people toward black people and started to ask questions about the converse. They began to ask, Who Riots? and Why?

The answers which they found to these two questions may be obvious to anyone who has been in close contact with community organizations or political groups in the black community. They were not obvious to persons who lacked such access or privileged communication, however, and the answers lend support to the notion that in order to understand intergroup relations we must consider *real* and not only relative deprivations.

In what follows we shall summarize the findings of numerous studies which have investigated the attributes and attitudes of persons who said that they either participated in, or approved of, the riots in cities across the United States. Like the seemingly paradoxical findings of earlier studies of relative deprivation, the black respondents who felt the riots were good and necessary were not people from the lowest rungs of our various ladders. They were *not* Marx's *lumpenproletariat* but people with higher incomes, more education, higher school grades, and higher needs for achievement; and their mothers tended to be more highly educated than were the mothers of people who disapproved of the riots (e.g., Caplan, 1970; Caplan & Paige, 1968; Forward & Williams, 1970; Sears & McConahay, 1970). They did not come from the ranks of the so-called hard-core unemployed but tended to move in and out of the labor force several times a year. They were more politically active and informed and held a greater number of organizational memberships than did their disapproving peers. They had a high sense of personal efficacy and power, but they also had a strong sense of the forces that thwarted their plans or behaviors.

From the description above, one might be tempted to conclude that this is one more instance which confirms relative deprivation theory or its less technical version—*the revolution of rising expectations.* But some aspects of that theory do not hold up on closer inspection of the data. The theory would predict, for instance, that riots occur when things are apparently getting better, but not quickly enough. As conditions become better, the theory says, people become more dissatisfied because the closer they come to the goal the more frustration they experience at not reaching the goal immediately. If this were true, one might expect the people who recently experienced the most progress to be the ones who riot. Yet there were no significant differences between the percentages of rioters and nonrioters who felt that things had recently gotten better or worse. The theory also predicts that those people who direct their anger against white society do so because they compare themselves with whites and feel relatively deprived. This again was not borne out by the data: Caplan and Paige (1968) found that *fewer* rioters (36 percent) than nonrioters (38 percent) felt that the black-white income gap was increasing, while *more* rioters (39 percent) than nonrioters (27 percent) felt the gap between rich and poor blacks was increasing.

Caplan and Paige went on to ask questions about the environmental constraints which the respondents sensed, and they found that the rioters or rebels were more aware of discrimination and reported having experienced it more often than their nonrebelling peers. While the rebels were more likely to say that black people are smarter, braver, and nicer than white people, they were also more angry with the *established* elements of American society, be they white or black. Thus, more than 50 percent of the rebels agreed with the statement, "Negroes who make a lot of money are just as bad as white people," while only 33 percent of the nonrebels agreed with this sentiment.

If the real source of discontent is social and economic inequality, and if the real "enemies" are the established wealthy segments of American society, why, one may ask, did the riots wreak havoc and destruction in poor black neighborhoods instead of on Madison Avenue or in Beverly Hills? The aggression, it appears, was displaced.

The factors that displaced the aggression are rather clear cut. It would have been difficult for the riot participants to approach the real centers of established American society and, even if they could have, it would have been prohibitively dangerous. The notion of displaced aggression is a well-founded phenomenon in psychological literature. It has been repeatedly found that aggression is displaced from the true source of frustration when there are prohibitions or heavy penalties for such aggression. Figure 3-2 gives a graphic representation of this. The tendency to be aggressive or hostile toward the true source of frustration is represented by the line labeled *approach.* The tendency to inhibit those actions or feelings is labeled *avoid.* Since the avoidance line is the steeper of the two, it effectively prevents action against the frustrating stimulus and displaces the aggression to some point further to the right—to a "safer" stimulus, which bears some similarity to the original one but which does not entail the same prohibitions or costs for acting on one's impulses.

Studies of displacement of human aggression have generally tried to demonstrate that aggression against frustrating in-group members (e.g., parents or members of one's inner circle) is inhibited and directed toward out-groups instead (e.g., Miller & Bugelski, 1948). It seems just as likely, however, that when out-groups do the frustrating (e.g., the police in Detroit or Newark) but are also powerful enough to make retaliation dangerous, aggression may again be displaced, and this time toward in-group members (e.g., small businessmen or home owners in black neighborhoods of those cities). This has been suggested as an explanation of the apparent self-hatred and the infliction of punishment on fellow pris-

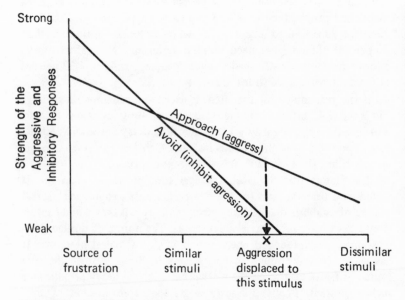

Figure 3-2 Displaced aggression as a result of the relationship between approach and avoidance gradients for aggressive acts.

oners that occurred among inmates of Nazi concentration camps, who released their aggression on one another because they dared not say a cross word to the prison guards (e.g., Bettleheim, 1943). Aggression is not always displaced, however, as we shall see later in this book; successful revolutions against oppressors do occur when the oppressed population risks the dangers of aggression against a powerful target.

We have so far examined two sources of group conflict and competition in this and the preceding chapter—real differences in opportunities or status and real differences in culture and social organization. In the following section we shall examine what happens when these two differences are combined, as they always have been in relations between the colonizers and the colonized. By heaping economic and status differences on cultural dissimilarities, colonialism represents perhaps the most explosive and extreme form of intergroup conflict, short of open warfare.

Colonialism: The Colonizer and the Colonized Earlier we cited examples of experimental studies in which intergroup tugs-of-war enhanced in-group solidarity and vice versa. Here we shall apply some of those analyses to the problems of colonialism. Lest it seem as though colonialism is a thing of the past or of faraway places, we shall try to demonstrate that black-white or Mexican-Anglo or French-English Canadian relations bear many of the characteristics of colonial relationships.

We also described several experiments in which fair competition in contests such as baseball games had quasi-therapeutic consequences for in-group morale. We want to examine the consequences of unfair competition, when the dice are loaded. While no quasi-colonial situations have been faithfully duplicated in laboratory experiments, some studies concerned with labor-management relations come the closest to examining the consequences of creating "winners" and "losers." Such a study was conducted by Blake and Mouton (1961), who instructed groups of adults to solve a complex problem.

They found, much like Sherif's Robber's Cave experiment, that the mere formation of distinct groups created a sense of consciousness and superiority of one's own group. Even before the competition began, the groups each rated themselves as above average when compared with the others. The introduction of competition enhanced these feelings, and led to distortions in judgment. Each group judged its own solutions or products superior to the products of the other groups. When the groups were permitted to ask questions of one another, each group focused upon the one that had been identified as its particular competitor, and they all asked questions whose answers would embarrass their adversaries.

When asked to describe the other group's position after the question period, each group exaggerated the differences between itself and its competitor and mistakenly assumed that the items which they both agreed on were part of their own group's solution alone. Finally, after winners and losers were identified, there were marked changes in the atmospheres of the two camps. The winners had a high sense of cooperation and work and were characterized by the researchers as "fat and happy." The losers, on the other hand, experienced high tension and tendencies toward fight or flight. They appeared to be "lean and hungry."

Since this experiment was done only once, we do not have a clear case of the dice being loaded. If the same groups had repeatedly won and lost, we would have a closer analogue to colonial relationships.

And if just one win-versus-loss created such distortions, attacks on the adversary, and consequences for morale, we get an inkling of what occurs with accumulated wins and losses.

While the problem has not been studied in scientific laboratories, we find abundant evidence of the consequences of such relationships in the accounts of colonialism offered by Franz Fanon (1965), Albert Memmi (1967), and Dominique Mannoni (1956). Each of these authors was a marginal member of either the colonized or colonizing groups in Africa. Fanon was a black Algerian psychiatrist educated in France, Memmi a Tunisian Jew who was a novelist and also educated in Paris, and Mannoni a European who spent many years in Madagascar. Moving closer to home, we may include the *Soledad Prison Letters* from George Jackson (1970), a black radical writer who was imprisoned at the age of eighteen and killed there at age thirty, and *The Autobiography of Malcolm X*, the black Muslim leader. No one of these accounts claims to be a social-psychological analysis of intergroup relations. Each, however, provides many years' and decades' worth of observations, self-reports, and case studies which we may read as data—no more or less biased than any other interviews or clinical or social observations used in social science. Since these observations come from highly charged situations, a reader may consider them less scientific than those coming out of isolated laboratories; but if we bear in mind the dilemmas discussed in Chapter 1, we shall recall that all social investigations reflect the values of their investigators, and what we must do is make those values explicit. The testimonies and observations which we describe do so quite openly.

The Colonizer and the Colonized: Intergroup Relationships of Unequal Power and Unfair Advantage   What is remarkable about all of the accounts which we have listed above is their common contention that the social situation creates the psychology of the individual rather than the reverse. This is a proposition which many social psychologists adhere to, and it is espoused in these polemical accounts as well as supported by experimental research. As subjective and value-laden as each of the books on colonialism is, it does not simply call the colonizers dirty names and suggest that they are the root of all evil. Instead, each one views the power holders and their subordinates alike as victims of an unequal relationship that brings out or creates the seemingly cruel and degraded characteristics with which we find them.

Portraits of the Colonizer We shall leave aside for this analysis those active colonizers who first set up the British East India Company or who commanded the conquering armies. They are relatively few in number compared with the great bulk of persons who followed them from their homelands to the colonies. The question that both Memmi and Mannoni ask concerning these followers is: Were they a select group of persons who sought power over others and who do not represent the "normal" homelander, or could what happened to them happen to any of us?

Memmi's portrait of the colonizer examines the choices open to persons who find themselves in a powerful and superior position. He asks first whether it is possible for a European to live in a colony without being singled out for special privileges. His answer is: "A colonial so defined does not exist, for all Europeans in the colonies are privileged" (p. 10).

> If he is in trouble with the law, the police and even justice will be more lenient toward him. If he needs assistance from the government, it will not be difficult; red tape will be cut; a window will be reserved for him where there is a shorter line so he will have a shorter wait. . . . Should he ask for or have need of anything, he need only show his face to be prejudged favorably. . . . He enjoys the preference of the colonized themselves, who grant him more than those who are the best of their own people. . . . From the time of his birth, he possesses a qualification independent of his personal merits or his actual class (p. 12).

Mannoni echoes a similar dilemma in that even the best-intentioned *ex-patriot*

> . . . finds the relationship ready made; he takes it up, adapts himself to it, and very often exploits it. And . . . whether he accepts it passively or seizes upon it greedily, the relationship changes him more than he it. It is precisely this transformation which sets a stamp on him which makes a colonial (p. 97).

One can hardly assume that the persons who do become colonials, living the lives of kings (or at least officials living at a higher rank than they would enjoy at home), represent a cross section of their homeland's population. Since homelanders are not randomly assigned to overseas jobs in colonies or former colonies, it is certainly conceivable that the people who are especially "power hungry" or "imperialistic" are attracted to such positions, and thus their own self-selection adds to their tendency to act as colonizers. We do have experimental evidence, however, which shows that even random assignment of normal college students to the positions of power-holder or subordinate can create effects similar to those observed in the colonizers.

A mock prison was created recently at Stanford University in which a group of student volunteers were assigned to be either "guards" or "prisoners" for a period of two weeks. The guards were given no specific instructions about the treatment of prisoners except to keep them in order. What emerged was a chamber of horrors that caused some prisoners to break down and terminate their part in the experiment after the first few days because of their extreme emotional reactions—rage, depression, acute anxiety, and fits of crying.

The prison "terms" were all abruptly cut short after six days because it was clearly harmful to both prisoners and guards to continue the relationship. Even those prisoners who did not break down and require immediate release in the first two days experienced the degradation:

"The way we were made to degrade ourselves really brought us down and that's why we all sat docile towards the end of the experiment."

"I learned that people can easily forget that others are human" (Haney et al., n.d., pp. 31–32).

And the consequences of the mock relationship were no less degrading for the guards—as seen in their self-reports:

"I was surprised at myself. . . . I made them call each other names and clean the toilets out with their bare hands. I practically considered the prisoners cattle, and I kept thinking I have to watch out for them in case they try something."

"During the inspection, I went to cell 2 to mess up a bed which the prisoner had made and he grabbed me, screaming that he had just made it, and he wasn't going to let me mess it up. He grabbed my throat, and although he was laughing I was pretty scared. I lashed out with my stick and hit him in the chin (although not very hard) and when I freed myself I became angry."

"I was tired of seeing the prisoners in their rags and smelling the strong odors of their bodies that filled the cells. I watched them tear at each other, on orders given by us."

". . . looking back, I am impressed by how little I felt for them" (Haney et al., n.d., pp. 30–31).

While the power of the guards degraded and devastated the prisoners, it appears to have corrupted the guards themselves, so that neither party emerged unscathed.

Another laboratory study addressed to the question, Does power corrupt? was conducted by a psychologist interested in the consequences of holding institutional powers (Kipnis, 1972). The subjects were college juniors and seniors who acted as mock managers; they were randomly assigned to positions of power or no-power. Their jobs were to supervise a supposed worker in the next room and to try to keep their production levels high for the sake of an imaginary company. The supervisers who were given "power" were told that they could communicate with their workers via a microphone and (1) promise to or actually reward the worker with ten-cent increases, (2) threaten to or actually transfer the worker to another job, and (3) threaten to or actually deduct ten cents per trial for poor work. The supervisors without power were merely asked to communicate with their workers over the microphone. All workers were to produce at the same rate, increasing their output over trials, so that the effects of holding power would be seen not in the workers' behavior but only in the supervisors' actions and attitudes. When Kipnis examined the actions of the two groups of supervisors, he found that while those without institutional resources relied on personal persuasion to influence their workers, those with the delegated powers made liberal use of those powers. They used persuasion only 16 percent of the time, and the rest of the time resorted to threats, promises, and actual meting out of rewards and punishments. Of even more interest than their actions per se are their attitudes. When asked to evaluate their workers' ability, worth, and deservingness, 72 percent of the supervisors with power rated their workers below average as compared with only 28 percent of the non-power-holding supervisors, although workers' behaviors were identical.

The discussion of these results by Kipnis, a social scientist, sounds not unlike the conclusions reached by Memmi and Mannoni, two observers of colonial scenes:

> . . . inequity in power is disruptive of harmonious social relations and drastically limits the possibilities that the power holder can maintain close and friendly relations with the less powerful. First of all, power increases the likelihood that the individual will attempt to influence and manipulate others. Second, the control of power appears to facilitate the development of a cognitive and perceptual system which serves to justify the use of power. That is, the subjects with power thought less of their subordinates' performance, viewed them as objects of manipulation, and expressed the desire to maintain social distance from them. . . . The more the subjects with power attempted to influence their workers, the less they wanted to meet them socially (pp. 39–40).

Portraits of the Colonized While the above descriptions focus on the consequences for the power holder, Memmi also provides a portrait of the colonized, and two black psychotherapists provide case histories of subordinated Americans in their study of black rage. Memmi writes:

> The fact is that the colonized does not govern. Being kept away from power, he ends up by losing both interest and feeling for control. How could he be interested in something from which he is so resolutely excluded? Among the colonized few men are suitable for government. How could such a long absence from autonomous government give rise to skill (p. 95)?

According to Memmi, the colonized person loses not only his interest in controlling the present but also his memory of his past:

> The memory which is assigned him is certainly not that of his people. The history which is taught him is not his own. He knows who Colbert or Cromwell was, but he learns nothing about Khaznadar; he knows about Joan of Arc, but not about El Kahena (p. 105).

And the powerless become weak: "What is clear is that colonization weakens the colonized and that all these weaknesses contribute to one another" (p. 115).

On quite another front, we learn from Grier and Cobbs (1968):

> Black men have stood so long in such peculiar jeopardy in America that a *black norm* has developed—a suspiciousness of one's environment which is necessary for survival. . . . it is a posture so close to paranoid thinking that the mental disorder into which black people most frequently fall is paranoid psychosis (p. 173).

In addition to such watchfulness, Grier and Cobbs repeatedly found a submerged condition of rage in the persons who sought therapy from them:

> An educated black woman had worked in an integrated setting for fifteen years. Compliant and deferential, she had earned promotions and pay increases by hard work and excellence. At no time had she been involved in black activism, and her only participation in the movement had been a yearly contribution to the NAACP.
>
> During a lull in the racial turmoil she sought psychiatric treatment. She explained that she had lately become alarmed at waves of rage that swept over her as she talked to white people or at times even as she looked at them. In view of her past history of compliance and passivity, she felt that something was wrong with her. If her controls slipped she might embarrass herself or lose her job (p. 174).

Grier and Cobbs ask, "Can we say that white men have driven black men mad?" (p. 173). In an allied field, a female psychologist, Phyllis Chesler, has written a book describing how men have driven some women crazy (1972).

The reader might wonder why we have relied here on writings and evidence which some might call more political than scientific. With the exception of Zimbardo's mock prison (and it was aborted prematurely), there are no laboratory studies of the consequences of being subordinate, powerless, discriminated against, or "driven mad." The mere suggestion of such research may indicate why it has not been done. Both the ethics of the profession and the sentiments of individual researchers prevent them from duplicating in the laboratory the harmful or humiliating conditions which have existed in some societies at some times in history. We must, therefore, rely on case histories and reports from participant-observers.

We have presented these portraits of the colonizers and the colonized (or in the current parlance, the oppressors and the oppressed) so that the reader may understand not only the historically documented instances of colonialism but also become aware of contemporary relationships which smack of paternalism and gross inequality. While the African, Indian, and other Asian nations are emerging into the post-colonial era, we may begin to see other instances of neocolonialism or previously unrecognized colonial-like relationships. Lest it appear that such caste relationships are ineradicable, however, we shall present a sociologist's analysis of the evolution of relationships from colonial to postcolonial—or in his terms, from paternalistic to competitive.

From Paternalism to Competition   The analysis which we present here comes from Pierre van den Berghe, a sociologist who was born in the Congo when it was still a Belgian colony and who has returned to Africa many times to study the evolution of race relations. The paternalistic relationship that is typified by colonialism is characterized not only by a highly unequal power relationship but also by the existence of distinct *castes* which have such great social distance between them that they permit minimal physical distance, even intimacy, without challenging the status inequalities. In the language we used earlier these leagues are so different that comparisons are not made between them and no one would ever expect to move from one to another. In competitive societies, on the other hand, class differences are more salient than caste distinctions; comparisons between groups or castes are permissible, and these comparisons give rise to much greater antagonism and hatred than paternalistic societies experience because the inequalities no longer seem legitimate.

We can summarize both the antecedents and consequences of these two systems of relations in Table 3-1.

If we examine race relations in the United States, the situation has clearly moved from the paternalism of the master-slave relationship to competition, with its consequently greater components of antagonism

Table 3-1   Nature of the Relationship Between Groups

I Antecedents	Paternalistic	Competitive
Economy	Agricultural; pastoral; nonindustrial	Large-scale industrial capitalism
Division of labor	Simple division of labor along racial (or caste) lines, with wide income gaps between castes	Complex division of labor according to "rational" criteria, not avowedly racial
Social Stratificatio	Caste system with a horizontal line between the higher and lower castes; no overlap in terms of social class	Caste system with a tilted line between castes so that there are some upper and lower classes in each, with considerable overlap
II Consequences		
Race relations	Accommodative, "benevolent" despotism	Antagonism; hatred
Segregation	Little physical segregation because status inequalities are so firm they are not threatened by physical closeness	Greater physical segregation
Psychological syndrome	Both groups believe in the subservient status of the lower caste and so no "need" for prejudice; pseudotolerance	A "need" for prejudice, with lynching, sadism, and scapegoating to justify the dominant group's response to the emerging competition
Stereotype of the lower caste	Childish, lazy, fun-loving, and inferior but lovable	Aggressive, insolent, despicable, inferior, and dangerous

Source: Adapted from P.L. van den Berghe, *Race and Racism: A Comparative Perspective, 1967.*

and hatred. To say that the relationship is now competitive is not to say that it is fair competition, however, for discrimination along racial or other lines sets limits on the competition and loads the dice against one

whole group of persons. Van den Berghe interjects his own values and beliefs in his final prognosis for race relations in America when he says that
the civil rights movements have only "called the bluff of nearly 200 years
of democratic rhetoric" (p. 93). He argues that the more fundamental
problems which require attention are the distribution of social rewards,
and the ownership and control of the means of production. Racism he
sees as a cosymptom rather than a cause of general social inequalities.

Van den Berghe's analysis has taken us up to the present in understanding the course of race relations in America and independence
movements in former colonies. We may well wonder where we will go
from here. We are still left with many unanswered questions.

Unanswered Questions

Will the old patterns of inequality give way to new and truly equal relationships? If social-psychological, utopian planners actually had the
power to redistribute resources such as money, power, status, educational opportunities, or desirable jobs, what would be the best way to
allocate such scarcities? We can certainly envision several different
grounds upon which allocation may be based—money or grades, for instance, may be allocated on the basis of performance or on the basis of
need. Allocations in a competitive society are presumably made on the
basis of performance (although we know that the correlation between
performance or "deservingness" and either money or grades is not perfect); and the distribution of goods in a pure communist or cooperative
society is presumably made on the basis of need (although we again
know that not everyone would agree on whose needs are greater and
whose lesser). Yet another method for dividing limited resources is to
use neither the competitive nor compensatory principle but the principle
of simple equality whereby each individual (or group) receives the same
quantity and quality of goods.

Even before answers to our questions may be attempted, it would
seem necessary first to establish the purposes for which our allocations
are to be made—the criteria by which we may evaluate the various distribution systems. Is our societal aim to promote happiness, to ensure
fairness and justice, to maximize efficiency, or all of the above? A long
line of research (e.g., Adams, 1965; Homans, 1961) suggests that we
tend to feel that rewards have been *fairly* allocated when all persons have
been rewarded according to their contributions or performances. Even
when such allocations are *un*equal (because the contributions or per-

formances are unequal), the result is considered *equitable* and therefore fair or just. But does equity translate into happiness? Or would the goal of maximizing happiness be better served by an equal rather than proportional distribution of rewards? Two social psychologists have dubbed this dilemma the problem of *hedonic relativism* and their analysis suggests that we still have a lot to learn about the consequences of various patterns of equality and inequality, equity and inequity (Brickman & Campbell, 1971).

Aside from the empirical issues and attempts at evaluating the effects of real and relative deprivations, we each undoubtedly have our own moral position about how the pie should be sliced. While competing hypotheses may be put to the test in the research arena, competing philosophies often remain forever at loggerheads. They are nonetheless worth debating, however, for we have seen in this chapter that inequality and privation can create unbearable life situations, and we are becoming increasingly aware that something's got to give.

Implications for Society

Even if we have not reached answers to the above questions, either as individuals or as a society, we do reach decisions each day which implicate us in the allocation process. Teachers give grades and students accept them—generally based on the principle of proportional equity (to each unto his abilities) rather than equality (to each unto his needs). Employers pay salaries and employees accept them—again generally based on the competitive model which is aimed at maximizing efficiency. Some communes have tried to divide their economic resources on the basis of need or strict equality; and some of these communities have survived for many generations (e.g., the Bruderhof) while others die out in a matter of months. Some schools have attempted to do away with grades and thereby eliminate one source of inequality, but most opt for the competitive model.

As we pointed out in Chapter 1, each one of us does operate on the basis of a value system which is often implicit, and presuming that we are neutral or undecided often amounts to supporting the status quo. It may behoove us to analyze the assumptions of our individual decisions, our family's traditions, our groups' philosophies, and our institutions' reward structures to make those values explicit and see whose side we are on when we discover real deprivations.

Chapter 4

Definitions of Groups: Symbolic Power and Social Roles

PROPOSITION

We inevitably lump people into groups and assign them roles, labels, and attributes as convenient simplifications of a complex social world. These definitions and attributions may have overwhelming consequences for the persons so labeled, so we speak of them as sources of symbolic power. Once attached, labels tend to persist, in spite of their errors, for they become self-fulfilling prophecies and thereby justify their own existence.

Illustrative Work

By social *labels* we mean a variety of descriptive tags which are attached to persons, such as idiot, or genius, male or female, liberal or conservative, black or white, and schizophrenic or normal, to name just a few. Any group or category name which enables us to classify persons into clusters which bear some social significance constitutes a social label of interest to us in this chapter. For a label to have some social significance, it must convey some additional information about the person beyond its own descriptive denotation. For instance, if someone is called brown-eyed that gives us no information about anything other than the color of the eyes and is not a social label of interest to us here. If, however, a person is called male or white, those labels convey more than the nature of the sex organ or the color of the skin, and they qualify as labels with "social significance."

The manner in which we shall treat such racial, sexual, and ethnic labels is derived from a sociological tradition often simply referred to as *labeling theory*. Labeling theory in sociology has been used primarily to understand problems of social deviance, and as such it may seem somewhat inappropriate for an analysis of intergroup relations. We shall try to show in the pages which follow, however, that the problems that beset persons classified as deviant are not, in fact, so different from the problems that beset persons who are sexually, racially, or ethnically categorized. In the sections which follow, we shall show how such social labels influence others' perceptions of the person and how this in turn influences the person's perception of him- or herself. We shall present some controversial data which suggest that labels not only influence our *perceptions* but actually *create* the attribute itself, with all of its behavioral manifestations. We will also examine methods which some groups have found to *resist* the attributions implied in their social labels and we will inquire into the apparent persistence or "stickiness" of social labels.

Labels and Symbolic Power: The Ability to Alter Others' Perceptions of Ourselves One fair day, eight "normal" persons admitted themselves into psychiatric wards of various hospitals under pseudonyms (Rosenhan, 1973). The pseudopatients changed only their names and occupations, but in all other respects tried to remain the same as they were on the outside. They were admitted by complaining that they had been hearing voices which said things like "empty," "hollow," and "thud," but once admitted they never complained of hearing voices again. Their purpose was to see whether they would be detected as normal, sane people who did not belong in psychiatric hospitals. Our purpose in mentioning this experiment is to show how the labels attached to these pseudopatients influenced the psychiatric staff's perceptions of them.

Since they had complained of hearing voices before entering the hospital, they received the dubious distinction of being called schizophrenic. Once having entered and been classified, however, they lost all symptoms of abnormality; they no longer heard voices and each person resumed his or her normal ways. Aside from being themselves, their only other assignment was to keep notes of the reactions they observed from the hospital staff and other patients. At first they were worried that they might be immediately detected as masqueraders, so they took great pains to keep their observations and note taking secret from the staff. It soon became apparent, however, that the staff took no notice of such behavior. In fact, the note taking itself became interpreted as one of their schizophrenic symptoms. One nurse wrote on her daily comment sheet, "Patient engages in writing behavior" (Rosenhan, 1973, p. 253).

It seems as though having "admitted" that they were schizophrenic by permitting themselves to be hospitalized, these pseudopatients could do nothing to prove themselves otherwise. Consider the following case history which one of the masqueraders revealed to a staff member and its subsequent translation by that staff member.

The case history as told by Rosenhan indicated that the masquerader

> . . . had a close relationship with his mother but was rather remote from his father during his early childhood. During adolescence and beyond, however, his father became a close friend, while his relationship with his mother cooled. His present relationship with his wife was characteristically close and warm. Apart from occasional angry exchanges, friction was minimal. The children had rarely been spanked. Surely there is nothing especially pathological about such a history (p. 253).

Compare this with the translation which appeared in the pseudopatient's case summary prepared by a staff member:

> This white 39-year-old male . . . manifests a long history of considerable ambivalence in close relationships, which begins in early childhood. A warm relationship with his mother cools during his adolescence. A distant relationship to his father is described as becoming very intense. Affective stability is absent. His attempts to control emotionality with his wife and children are punctuated by angry outbursts and, in the case of the children, spankings. And while he says that he has several good friends, one senses considerable ambivalence embedded in those relationships also . . . (p. 253).

The patient's diagnosis as schizophrenic so tainted all of his behaviors past and present that it would seem there was no way for him out of the hospital. The more he claimed to be well, the more disturbed he might have been considered.

Ironically, while the diagnostic label schizophrenic was believed and accepted by the psychiatric staff it did not fool fellow patients. Some of the "real" patients who encountered the masqueraders detected them immediately and said things like: "You're not crazy. You're a journalist, or a professor [referring to the continual note taking]. You're checking up on the hospital" (Rosenhan, 1973, p. 252). While these patients saw through the disguise immediately, the psychiatric staff never perceived the pseudopatients as normal, even when they were finally discharged, for their discharges all bore the inscription "schizophrenia in remission," implying that they might someday return. Rosenhan concludes:

> A psychiatric label has a life and an influence of its own. Once the impression has been formed that the patient is schizophrenic, the expectation is that he will continue to be schizophrenic. When a sufficient amount of time has passed, during which the patient has done nothing bizarre, he is considered to be in remission and available for discharge. But the label endures beyond discharge, with the unconfirmed expectation that he will behave as a schizophrenic again (p. 253).

Our reason for dwelling on this case is to let our readers become thoroughly skeptical about the validity of one set of psychodiagnostic labels with the hope that this skepticism might now be transferred to other psycho- or sociodiagnostic labels. Among the other labels which we consider to be as potentially "errorful" and influential as the schizophrenic tag are those which designate persons as black or white, and male or female. In order to demonstrate this, however, we would have to perform a much more difficult experiment than Rosenhan's. We would have to take a white man, color his skin black (or vice versa), and send him into the world with instructions to behave as he always has. Our measure of the power of his new label to influence the perceptions of others would consist of interviews with observers asked to comment about his essential "whiteness" or "blackness." While such a study would certainly be difficult to carry out on a large scale, an experimenting novelist did precisely this, and recorded his experiences in a book entitled *Black Like Me* (Griffin, 1962).

J. H. Griffin was a Southern white journalist who, much like Rosenhan's accomplices, decided to see what it would be like to be treated as though he were a black man. Like the pseudopatients, he changed only a superficial aspect of his being and observed how every action was reinterpreted by others in light of his new identity. He shaved his hair and darkened his skin and then ventured forth into the world of Louisiana and Mississippi. His attempt at "passing" was even more successful than the pseudopatients', for no one suspected his true color, not even the black people among whom he found refuge and friendship. Whatever it was that black people were assumed to possess to justify the hate stares and the restrictions For Whites Only, he apparently possessed by virtue of his new skin. Unusual sexual powers and customs were also assumed to accompany his skin color, for he was subjected to endless questioning about his sex life while hitchhiking with local white citizens.

The interesting point which both Rosenhan's and Griffin's experiments raise is this: If the social world with which these masqueraders were in contact *erred* by falsely attributing inner qualities to the pseudopatients and pseudoblack person, what prevents the same social world from having erred in its attributions to "real" patients or "real" black men? Rosenhan (1973) has some evidence that a good number of "real" patients may in fact be "normals" who have been falsely diagnosed and classified as "schizophrenic." He told some hospital staff members that at some time during the next three months one or more pseudopatients would try to be admitted to the hospital. At the end of the three months, he asked the staff to guess which of the 193 patients admitted during that time were "normals" who were passing as patients. His data, shown in the following table, are both encouraging and terrifying:

No. of patients alleged to be pseudopatients	Allegation made by:
41	At least one member of the staff
23	At least one psychiatrist
19	One psychiatrist *and* one other staff member

In actuality, not one pseudopatient had tried to gain admission during those three months. What is encouraging about the data is the possibility that these staff members could detect, and in nineteen cases even agree upon, the essential "normality" of some of the patients. What is, by the same token, terrifying about the data is the likelihood that those nineteen cases and many others like them may remain hospitalized because no one has hinted that they may be pseudopatients or questioned the veridicality of their diagnosis.

In theory, we might employ a similar detection experiment to see how many males have been misclassified as "masculine" and females as "feminine." In practice, this has been done by female impersonators, who trick the unwary into believing they are talking with a truly beautiful feminine woman who then turns out to be a man in reality (Greenhaus, 1973). Yet while Rosenhan's experiment makes us doubt the validity of our classification system of normals and schizophrenics, female impersonators make us doubt not our own system of classifying persons into male and female but the normality of morality of that particular impersonator instead. For some reason a person's sex role does not appear to be as open to negotiation as does his normality, perhaps because sex approaches what the sociologist Everett Hughes (1958) calls a "master status," one that is more permanent and powerful than all others. If men, on the average, appear more masculine than women, we may still ask, however, whether it is "in their nature" or whether they too have been persuaded by their labels. This is the question we shall address in the following section.

Labels and Symbolic Power: The Ability to Alter Our Own Attributes and Behaviors An early sociologist by the name of George Horton Cooley coined the phrase *looking-glass self* to refer to the fact that our own conceptions of ourselves are largely a reflection of what other people around us say and think about us. Our habits and manners strike those around us in particular ways and their reactions affect how we think of ourselves. If our social tags or labels affect others' perceptions of our attributes and abilities, they are bound to become part of our own self-concept through this indirect route of reflection. The consequences of this labeling process are thus often referred to as a self-fulfilling prophecy, as demonstrated in the following experiment by two psychologists.

Robert Rosenthal and Lenore Jacobson (1968) entered an elementary school in California and explained to the teachers that they were engaged in an important piece of research on intelligence testing. They told the teachers:

All children show hills, plateaus, and valleys in their scholastic progress. The study being conducted at Harvard with the support of the National Science Foundation is interested in those children who show an unusual forward spurt of academic progress. These spurts can and do occur at any level of academic and intellectual functioning. When these spurts occur in children who have not been functioning too well academically, the result is familiarly referred to as "late blooming."

As a part of our study we are further validating a test which predicts the likelihood that a child will show an inflection point or "spurt" within the near future. This test which will be administered in your school will allow us to predict which youngsters are most likely to show an academic spurt. The top 20 percent (approximately) of the scorers on this test will probably be found at various levels of academic functioning.

The development of the test for predicting inflections or "spurts" is not yet such that *every* one of the top 20 percent will show the spurt or "blooming" effect. But the top 20 percent of the children *will* show a more significant inflection or spurt in their learning within the next year or less than will the remaining 80 percent of the children (p. 66).

They recorded the children's grades and IQ scores in September and again the following May. The results, particularly for first and second graders, were what you might have predicted: the bloomers gained in both grades and IQ much more than the nonbloomers did. The graph on the following page depicts their IQ score improvement. The predicted spurts for "bloomers" were most pronounced in the early grades. For these children it would seem that the Harvard Test of Inflected Acquisition was a good predictor.

Now imagine the teachers' faces when they were told that the test was a hoax. There was no such thing as a Harvard Inflected Acquisition test, nor were there any real bloomers. Instead, the experimenters had randomly assigned 20 percent of the children to the bloomer category. They had in effect pulled names out of a hat, and the lucky 20 percent whose names were pulled benefited. How? you may rightly ask.

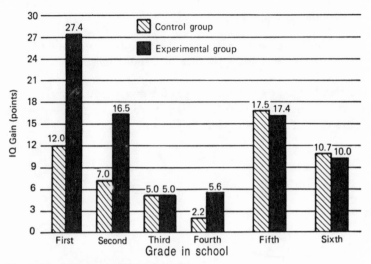

Figure 4-1 Gains in total IQ in six grades.

The teachers were not instructed to treat those bloomers differently. They received no special classes or extra material. All that the teachers were told was to *expect* them to bloom by the end of the year.

Social scientists have long been aware of the role of expectations in shaping another's behavior, indeed even his concept of *self* (see especially Mead, 1934). The way others' expectations work has long been as elusive as stardust, however, and it is now only beginning to be explained. When psychologists tackle complex questions, they often step back to the level of rats, hoping that the greater control and simplicity of that organism's life history will afford some answers. Let us do the same.

Rosenthal (1966) reports a labeling study with rats in which a group of college students were led to believe that through generations of selective breeding it has been possible to produce pure strains of maze-bright and maze-dull rats. One group of students was instructed:

> Those of you who are assigned the Maze-Bright rats should find your animals on the average showing some evidence of learning during the first day of running. Thereafter performance should rapidly increase (p. 159).

The other group was told:

Those of you who are assigned the Maze-Dull rats should find on the average very little evidence of learning in your rats (p. 159).

The results were as they should be—the maze-bright animals outperformed the maze-dull rats, and this difference increased over the successive days of the experiment. (See Figure 4-2.)

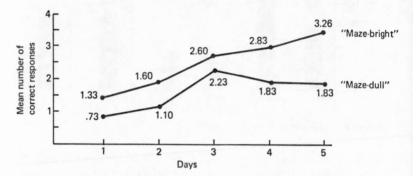

Figure 4-1 Maze learning of so-called bright and dull rats. *(Adapted from Rosenthal, 1966, p. 161.)*

The punch line here is the same as for the study of the children who "bloomed": there were no maze-bright or maze-dull animals. They all came from the same pool and were randomly assigned to the categories. All differences which appeared in their learning skills were differences created by the experimenters' *expectations*.

Again, the experimenter-teachers were not told to treat "bright" animals differently from "dull" ones, but there is nonetheless evidence that they did. At the end of the learning trials, the experimenters were asked to describe their own behavior. They rated themselves on how satisfied, relaxed, pleasant, friendly, enthusiastic, and talkative they were, and on how much they handled their animals. This study, and succeeding ones on similarly counterfeit Skinner-Box-Bright and Skinner-Box-Dull rats, suggest important differences in how the experimenters felt and acted toward their rats. Those who believed their animals to be bright were more satisfied, relaxed, pleasant, and friendly, and they apparently handled their animals more. Gentle handling for laboratory rats may be analogous to cuddling for children, or to giving a pat on the head. In any case, it is positively reinforcing. Rosenthal explains that "experimenters expecting good performance may have rewarded their rats tactually after a good performance, and such reward may have improved the animals' performance in the subsequent experiment [or trial]" (p. 174). In addition, experimenters with the "bright" rats watched their animals more closely than did those with the "dull" animals. Anyone who has tried to train a dog to do tricks or a rat to press a lever knows that careful observation is essential for shaping the animal's behavior. Finally, 47 percent of the students stuck with the so-called dull rats made spontaneous comments about the *uneducability* of their animals, while only 5 percent of the students with "bright" rats made such disparaging remarks. The trainers of the "dull" animals were so convinced of the stupidity of their subjects that when the random feature of the experiment was explained to them, they persisted in their belief that *their* animals were especially dull.

> Many of these experimenters point out that, of course, by random sampling, the two groups of rats would not differ *on the average*. However, they continued, under random sampling, some of the "dull" rats would really be dull by chance and that *their* animal was a perfect example of such a phenomenon (p. 176).

Rosenthal's work has some disturbing implications. It questions whether children's IQ scores reflect the child's ability or the teacher's *beliefs* about the child's ability. The publication of his work has understandably generated a large number of related studies, many of them trying to test the reliability of such expectancy effects. We shall mention some unsuccessful as well as successful replications of the *Pygmalion effect*.

One group of investigators reports five unsuccessful attempts to replicate the experimenter-bias effect in laboratory studies (Barber et al., 1969). A critical review of thirty-one studies which Rosenthal has cited as support of experimenter-expectancy effects demonstrates that many of the studies used inappropriate statistical techniques; others report findings that might be due to chance (Barber & Silver, 1968). A few studies have tried to replicate the Pygmalion effect in classrooms and they too have failed. When studies obtain no results, however, it is never clear whether the fault lies with the theory (Rosenthal's, in this case) or with the experiment that failed to produce significant results. For instance, one classroom study that failed to find a significant increase in pupils' IQ after teachers were told that some students would bloom also found that 61 percent of the teachers stated that they had *not expected* the children to show improvement as a result of their bloomers' test scores (Jose & Cody, 1971). This hardly seems like a test of expectancy effects, then, if the teachers never formed positive expectancies in the first place.

Other classroom studies report results that confirm Rosenthal's hypothesis (e.g., Beez, 1968; Meichenbaum et al., 1969; Seaver, 1973). One of these found that your fate may be sealed not only by what your teachers think of you, but also by what they think of your older brothers or sisters, if you are unlucky enough to have the same teacher. If an older sibling does well, teachers expect the younger sibling to do just as well, and if the first failed, teachers expect the second to follow suit (Seaver, 1973). Critics might argue that siblings are naturally going to perform similarly because they have similar genes and upbringings. Seaver points out that the similarities are exaggerated, however, by having the same teacher, who imposes the same expectations on the second that he acquired from the first: Here comes another one of those Joneses!

In the studies reported above, we have seen how often others' expectations may actually create in us those attributes which they expect us to possess, such as intelligence (and presumably also stupidity). These studies report no direct evidence that the teachers' or experimenters' expectations influenced what the children thought of themselves, though presumably after the children saw their own grades or IQ scores rise, they too came to believe that they were bright.

J. H. Griffin's experiment in passing for black presents more direct evidence of the influence of his label on his own view of himself. He internalized the code, Thou shalt not look longingly at a white woman, to such an extent that at times he could not bring himself to call or write to his wife, for she was white and thus out of his reach.

In several of the experiments we have discussed so far, there was an end in sight to the identities temporarily adopted. Rosenhan's pseudo-patients knew they would eventually be released from their confinement and Griffin knew he could become "white" soon after he stopped taking the medication. The emotional and cognitive changes brought on by their respective labels wore off when the persons were released from their roles. When the term is indefinite or endless, however, the personal effects persist, and the identity with which a person is saddled becomes the real self, for there is no other in sight.

Observations of the prisoners in World War II concentration camps (e.g., Bettleheim, 1943) suggest that the camps became the real world for the inmates. Their former identities were lost, old occupations meant nothing, and speaking of someone as "a lawyer from Toulouse" seemed absurd (Elkins, 1959). Such former titles were irrelevant because there was no future outside the camps, and those statuses were lost forever.

> [A] factor having deep disintegrative effects upon the prisoner was the prospect of a limitless future in the camp. In the immediate sense this meant that he could no longer make plans for the future. But there would eventually be a subtler meaning: it made the break with the outside world a *real* break; in time the "real" life would become the life of the camp, the outside world an abstraction. Had it been a limited detention, whose end could be calculated, one's outside relationships—one's roles, one's very "personality"—might temporarily have been laid aside, to be reclaimed more or less intact at the end of the term. Here, however, the prisoner was faced with the apparent impossibility of his old roles or even his old personality ever having any future at all; it became more and more difficult to imagine himself resuming them (Elkins, 1959, pp. 107–108).

Elkins (1959) likens slavery in the United States to imprisonment in the concentration camps of Germany. Both stripped those who entered of their former identities—clothing, names, and statuses—both had involuntary confinement; and both meted out indefinite or life (and death) sentences. Slaves, moreover had not only a life sentence for themselves, but for their children, grandchildren, and as far as they could see into the future. The slaves who were transported from Africa to the United States, therefore, lost their former personalities and identities for similar reasons. With no release in sight, their having been prosperous farmers or merchants in West Africa became irrelevant. They became what they played at in Virginia—slaves with no names, no histories, no futures. Elkins therefore sees the so-called Sambo personality as an undeniable development, a fulfillment of a role become real.

Most studies that have demonstrated the effects of expectations have been performed either in laboratories, hospitals, concentration camps, or classrooms. All are restricted environments where the subjects are closely watched and controlled by monitors. Would we find the same labeling effects in the outside world? Sociologists say yes, and they illustrate their case with data on juvenile "delinquents," adult "criminals," and other rule breakers (Becker, 1963; Wheeler et al., 1969). Applying the delinquent label or ". . . official stamp may help to organize responses different from those that would have arisen without the official action" (Wheeler et al., p. 609). Further, say these authors:

> Their association with others who are similarly defined may make the category "delinquent" or "criminal" much more salient for them as well as for others' views of them. In other words, the individual begins to think of himself as delinquent, and he organizes his behavior accordingly (p. 609).

An illustration of this process appears in the account of "The Saints and the Roughnecks," as told by William Chambliss (1973). Chambliss recorded the truancy and delinquency of two groups of high school boys whom he dubbed Saints and Roughnecks. In terms of the sheer number of delinquent acts, the Saints actually topped the Roughnecks, because they successfully escaped from school more frequently, more often drove while drunk, and engaged in petty vandalism on their drives around town on Saturday nights. Yet the Roughnecks were regarded as more delinquent by the local police and residents, because when they were drunk, they were not out in cars but rather hanging around the corner tavern, and when they stole it was not from construction projects at the edge of town but from the local merchants. The Roughnecks were more visible, less repentant, and less wealthy than the Saints, all of which contributed to their being perceived as a greater problem. As a result, observes Chambliss:

> The community responded to the Roughnecks as boys in trouble, and the boys agreed with that perception. Their pattern of deviancy was reinforced, and breaking away from it became increasingly unlikely. Once the boys acquired an image of themselves as deviants, they selected new friends who affirmed that self-image.

Even outside walled institutions, therefore, labels take effect. Is it not possible to argue, then, that seemingly natural category names like male or female, black or white are also "official stamps which help to organize responses different from those that would have arisen without the official action"? Is it not possible that society's expectations of how boys should behave have shaped the attitudes and behavior of people called *boys* just as the teachers' expectations of "bloomers" shaped their performance? Similarly, expectations of what black people are like have shaped the personalities and performance of black individuals. The Black Power movement of the 1960s was a move to change those expectations and concepts. What that movement has done is substitute a positive set of labels for a negative set. It still maintains, indeed strengthens, the notion that there is special significance to being black—rather than to *being thought of as* black.

Methods for Resisting the Attributions Implied in Social Labels
The notion, "This is what it is like to *be thought of as* X" rather than, "This is what it is like to *be* X" might enable persons to resist accepting the social attributions. Consciousness-raising groups stress the former and teach their members that many of their attributes are not a function of what they are but of what they are thought of as being. Other groups succeed in never accepting the attribution in the first place. Some boys who engage in homosexual prostitution for an income, for instance, know that they may *be thought of as* "queer," but they and their peers know they *are not* (Riess, 1964). Some persons with physical handicaps know they are as normal as their neighbors, and they may even notice some handicaps in so-called normals:

> Both healthy minds and healthy bodies may be crippled. The fact that "normal" people can get around, can see, can hear, doesn't mean that they are seeing or hearing. They can be very blind to the things that spoil their happiness, very deaf to the pleas of others for kindness; when I think of them I do not feel any more crippled or disabled than they. Perhaps in some small way I can be the means of opening their eyes to the beauties around us: things like a warm handclasp, a voice that is anxious to cheer, a spring breeze, music to listen to, a friendly nod. These people are important to me, and I like to feel that I can help them. (Written by a person with multiple sclerosis in Goffman, 1963, p. 11.)

What irks people who are stigmatized for one handicap is the tendency for "normals" to attribute other handicaps to them. Someone who cannot see is often shouted at, as though he could not hear either. Someone who cannot hear is often thought of as lacking intelligence too. Sometimes "normals" err in the other direction too, and assume that a person who lacks one sense must have a superior ability in other senses, as when a sightless person is asked to test perfumes. The stigmatized persons know full well that these other attributions are wrong, and it may be that these additional errors enable them to reject the stigmatizing view that "normals" have of them.

Other mechanisms which enable one group to reject the attributions made by another are claiming ignorance of one's condition and disowning responsibility for the behavior. Those "good" Germans who lived in Germany during the period of the concentration camps are an example. A sociologist, Everett Hughes (1964), visited postwar Germany in 1948 and found himself asking, "How could such dirty work be done among and, in a sense, *by* the millions of ordinary, civilized German people?" (1962, p. 4). He concludes that Germans are no different from the rest of us in ability to perform evil. Nor do they think of themselves as bad people. Rather, those with whom he spoke said they knew little of what was happening in the concentration camps. That dirty work was being done by a secret society (the SS troups) which had a mandate to deal with "the Jewish problem." Such a division of labor lets both parties off the hook. Those not involved can remain ignorant of the brute facts, and those with the mandate can say their acts were sanctioned by others. It needs little imagination to see that this happens not only in Germany. The American public was indeed ignorant of the My Lai massacre until many months after it happened; and the soldiers involved said they were merely obeying orders and doing a job that the American public had sanctioned. People who kill as members of an organization like the army always feel they have permission, and their acts thus reflect not on them as individuals but on the nature of their job (Sanford et al., 1971). The public which gives them permission maintains its innocence in other ways—by being ignorant of the facts, by dehumanizing the victims, and by believing that the well-being of their nation depends on the actions of that organization (Sanford et al., chap. 3). It would seem that wide newspaper and television coverage of today's wars would not allow the "good" people to remain ignorant for long. *Selective* reporting and televising, however, can serve to further dehumanize the enemies and the victims by showing only their atrocities and not ours.

Judges and hangmen are also good men engaged in dirty work. They may sentence murderers to death and tie the ropes around their necks without, in the process, becoming murderers themselves. It is part of their job and if they did not do it, someone else would. The public, accordingly, does not hold them responsible. Their actions reflect not on themselves but on the requirements of a role.

In the case of judges, soldiers, and hangmen, there is no attributional problem. The public has already given them a sanction, so neither they nor the public make an attribution of responsibility in the first place. In the case of stigmatized groups, there is a problem of resisting the attributions made by others.

Just as some stigmatized groups resist the attributions of "queer," "deaf," or "disabled," so some other minority groups have learned to resist society's negative expectations. Several studies of the self-esteem of "culturally disadvantaged" children (black, Puerto Rican, and white children from families with an income less than four thousand dollars) show that these children have significantly higher self-esteem ratings than their more advantaged peers (Soares & Soares, 1969, 1971). The mechanism whereby they resist attributing their economic disadvantages to some personal shortcoming may be similar to the mechanism used by the soldiers, judges, and other good people—namely, placing the responsibility for their position on someone else's shoulders. There is some evidence that radical black youth do this—rather than attribute their position in life to their personal skills or efforts, they attribute it to the system of racial discrimination (Gurin et al., 1969). If they attribute failures to the system and successes to themselves, the reasoning may go: I have gotten this far in spite of such systematic discrimination, imagine how far I could go with a fair chance.

The Imperfections in Social Labels Social categories are imperfect in several ways. First, the rules for categorizing persons are not uniformly applied. For instance, if one boy throws a brick through a window, he may be severely scolded by his parents, perhaps have his allowance or car privileges reduced, but in the end be dismissed under the old rule that boys will be boys. If another boy, however, who has neither an allowance nor car privileges, throws the same brick through the same window, he may be taken to court as another "juvenile delinquent" (Chambliss, 1973). This biased application of a rule and its label is particularly common in the area of deviance.

> Since deviance is, among other things, a consequence of the responses of others to a person's act, students of deviance cannot assume that they are dealing with a homogeneous category when they study people who have been labeled deviant. That is, they cannot assume that these people have actually committed a deviant act or broken some rule, because the process of labeling may not be infallible; some people may be labeled deviant who in fact have not broken a rule. Furthermore, they cannot assume that the category of those labeled deviant will contain all those who actually have broken a rule, for many offenders may escape apprehension and thus fail to be included in the population of "deviants" they study. Insofar as the category lacks homogeneity and fails to include all the cases that belong in it, one cannot reasonably expect to find common factors of personality or life situation that will account for the supposed deviance (Becker, 1963, p. 9).

People who habitually take paper, pens, pencils, and other office supplies for home use are not thought of as stealing even though they make it a regular habit. A boy on a one-time shoplifting spree, however, may be apprehended and marched off to court for stealing, even though it was more likely a temporary phase in his life.

A second imperfection in labels is the lack of fit occasionally found between social and personal definitions. The following table illustrates this:

| | Social label or definition | |
	Normal; good	Stigmatized; bad
Personal label or definition		
Normal; good	(Agreement)	(Error) Passing or rejecting
Stigmatized; bad	(Error) Passing or rejecting	(Agreement)

All of the experiments described earlier on the consequences of labels were studies of people who were passing. The psychologist, Rosenhan, passed as a mental patient; Griffin, a white man, passed as a black man; an average group of students passed as bloomers; and normal rats passed as either bright or dull. The point of all these experiments was, of course, to show how a social definition becomes a personal definition; how what others think of a person affects how he thinks of himself. Some other studies, however, demonstrated the ability of some people to reject others' definitions of themselves—to maintain a positive self-concept, for instance, in the face of society's negative evaluations.

According to one school of social psychological thought, what determines whether or not a person *accepts* his social label is what his *significant others* think (Mead, 1934). Significant others may be parents, friends, colleagues, or someone like a teacher, scout leader, or another avuncular figure, or they may be fellow inmates, partners in crime, and other stigmatized people. In short, they are those people whose opinions a person cares about.

The Black-Is-Beautiful movement, for instance, established a group of significant others—other blacks instead of whites—who redefined many aspects of black culture and identity. This enabled individuals to reject the larger society's long-standing definitions of black as evil or ugly. Similarly, the women's liberation movement has established new definitions of womanhood which include careers, assertiveness, independence, and the traditional manly virtues such as courage, ambition, and strength. Those women who identify with the movement have learned to reject the traditional definitions of themselves; those whose significant others do not share the movement's ideas see no discrepancy between their own and society's definitions. Whenever there is a lack of fit, each could say the other is wrong. Liberated women say American society's definitions of womanhood are unconscionable; traditional American society says liberated women are unnatural.

In some instances, the disagreement is not over the attributes of a sex but over the sex itself. Everyone has probably heard of a person who decides that he or she was misclassified in childhood—that instead of a male, she is really a female, or vice versa. Research done at Johns Hopkins University (Money & Ehrhardt, 1972) on transsexuals and others of ambiguous sexual identity even points to real physiological mechanisms that may underlie this conviction: The sexual morphology (i.e., body appearance) of a child is fully elaborated before the hormones produced by sex organs circulate to the part of the brain (the hypothalamus) that later becomes a governing mechanism in the production of predominantly male or predominantly female hormones. If, as is sometimes thought to be the case, something interferes with the uptake of those hormones, then the result can be a child whose "brain chemistry" has not kept sexual pace with his morphology. Money and his colleagues have pointed out that the reason there are so many more male-to-female transsexuals also makes embryological sense: The basic, undifferentiated human embryo, regardless of *genetic* constitution, will develop chemically and morphologically into a female unless the predominantly male hormones (testosterone and androgen) are added in sufficient quantity at the right time. Thus the male-to-female transsexual is said to be a genetic male whose prenatal hormonal uptake proceeded normally to the point of morphological differentiation, but somehow got cut off at those later stages of fetal development when the circulation of sex hormones in the brain may be crucial to later psychosexual self-identity as a male. Hence the feeling of so many would-be transsexuals that they are "females trapped in male bodies."

While the transsexual says that society was just plain wrong about his identity, society tends to call the person's preferences perverted—particularly since the would-be transsexual so often "looks like" such an ordinary male in all other respects. But even more equivocal misclassifications can occur when a child who is genetically of one sex appears at birth to be morphologically of the opposite sex. In the case of a female misclassified as a male, this can be due to an overproduction of male hormones in embryo. (It is important to note that both "male" and "female" hormones are present in both sexes; it is the *relative* amounts of each that produce the morphology of one sex or the other.) In the case of the male misclassified as a female, it can be due to an underproduction of male hormones, or a cellular inability to take up those hormones which are produced—in this case the inability occurring at a much earlier stage of fetal development than in the case of the transsexual whose body has been differentiated as male, but whose brain has not. Once these "misclassified" males or females reach puberty, the development of secondary sex characteristics starts to give the real story away, and some kind of decision must be made regarding what kind of sex surgery to undertake: restoration of the *genetic* sex (which is starting to assert itself in secondary sex characteristics) or encouragement by hormone therapy of the up-to-now socialized or *labeled* sex. It is of interest that the overwhelming majority of these "ambiguous" children opt for the sex in which they were raised, thus demonstrating that labeling and its attendant social consequences are strong competitors for the biology-is-destiny theory. But lest we totally ignore the possible weight of biological factors in self-identity, let us remember that, more often than not, the male-to-female transsexual looks like, and has been raised as, a perfectly ordinary male child—yet *still* feels like a "female trapped in a male body," thus making Money's explanation of interrupted brain-hormone circulation at least plausible in such instances.

A third imperfection in the system of labels (though imperfection is too weak a word here) concerns their correctness in a moral or ethical sense. "To deal with a human being exclusively *qua* 'Negro' is an act of 'bad faith,' no matter whether these dealings are those of a racist or a racial liberal" (Berger, 1963, p. 157). Even replacing the negative labels with positive ones does not eliminate this moral dilemma.

> . . . those on the receiving end of negative identity assignments are very prone to accept the categories invented by their oppressors with the simple alteration of replacing the minus sign originally attached to the identity in question with a plus sign. Jewish reactions to anti-Semitism furnish classic illustrations of this process, with the Jewish counter-definitions of their own identity simply reversing the signs attached to the anti-Semitic categories without fundamentally challenging the categories themselves. . . . enjoining upon the Negro "pride of race" . . . is but a shadow of its white prototype. . . . This is not to deny that counterformations such as the ones mentioned may be functional in organizing resistance to oppression and may have a certain political validity much like other myths. All the same, they are rooted in "bad faith," the corrosive power of which eventually exacts its toll as those who have painfully acquired "pride of race" discover that their acquisition is a hollow one indeed (Berger, pp. 157–158).

The Persistence of Social Labels If social labels are so errorful and if some groups have been able to find ways to resist or refute their attributions, why do they still persist? And once applied, why do they adhere or appear to be so "sticky"?

We tend to hold persons rather than circumstances responsible for their characteristics. Our common-sense psychology says that if a twig is bent, it is because the wind blew, but if a person acts crooked it is likely due to his crooked nature (Heider, 1958). If there is some obvious force which bends a person as the wind bends a twig, we do acknowledge that. The problems lie in the nonobvious character of many social forces.

Studies in person perception have found that we sometimes utilize contradictions and exceptions to the rule in making judgments of people. When a person's behavior is inconsistent with his or her prescribed role, we assume that behavior tells us something about the person. A person applying for a job as an astronaut, for instance, is expected to act like an astronaut. If he does, it tells us little about his own personality. If he does not conform to expectations, however, we feel that we have gotten a glimpse of the real John Doe. "The most probable inference from role departures . . . is that the person reveals something of his 'true self' through his failure to perform the expected role" (Jones et al., 1961, p. 303). If a professor acts professorially, a nurse acts nurturantly, or a politician acts politically, we do not know what the real person is like. But when they act in ways inconsistent with their official roles, they reveal something of themselves.

According to this reasoning, if a woman acts womanly, it does not tell us anything about herself but merely reflects her role. We should dismiss her feminine behaviors as nothing but role requirements. Our naive psychologizing does not make the same allowances for being male or female, however, that it makes for being an astronaut. When a man acts manly, we do not suspend judgment and say, "I really don't know what he's like because he's acting the way he's supposed to." Instead, we assume, "He's a real man!" The role requirements for men and women apparently do not seem to be as binding or external as do other occupational roles.

Similarly for the roles of black and white. When white people act the way we expect white people to act, we do not attribute their behavior to external forces and role expectations but rather to something about white people—perhaps the essence of whiteness. From a social-psychological standpoint, racial roles and sexual roles have as many requirements and external forces working on the players as do occupational roles. These external constraints may even be stronger. The naive perceiver, however, fails to recognize such external forces and instead attributes the performances to the essence of blackness, whiteness, maleness, and so on.

The same is true for making inferences about ourselves. We weigh the apparent external forces acting upon us and, if there seem to be few, we attribute the action to our own selves—our wishes, motives, and attitudes (e.g., Bem, 1967; Festinger, 1957; Schachter & Singer, 1962). In the process of self-perception as well as in the process of social attribution, naive perceivers fail to recognize the external forces, requirements, and demands of social roles.

We must, therefore, make an amendment to the law that behavior consistent with a role is discounted and behavior inconsistent with a role is credited to the individual: We utilize inconsistencies between what is expected and what a person does when we make judgments about *dynamic* qualities of the person such as his motivation, aggressiveness, and attitudes (Kepka & Brickman, 1971). When judging what are thought to be more static *structural* qualities, however, we treat inconsistencies as though they were freak occurrences. If a student appears to have low ability, for instance, but suddenly does well, a teacher is more likely to attribute this sudden success to good teaching rather than to the student's intelligence (Johnson et al., 1964). When that same student does poorly, however, the teacher transfers responsibility to the student rather than attribute the performance to poor teaching. This poor student is damned if he does and damned if he doesn't, because his failing is assumed to be a structural defect.

Occasionally, a book, a lecture, or a demonstration in social psychology can liberate a person from his or her role and make it clear that the person has developed ways of being and thinking because a role has required it. More often, however, it requires a dose of radical therapy to teach people not to attribute undesirable habits to their *selves* but rather to society or the system.[1]

A modified version of such radical therapy has been prescribed for society as a whole by B. F. Skinner in his book *Beyond Freedom and Dignity* (1971). He advocates attributing all events to environmental contingencies rather than blaming or praising individuals. This message has met great resistance because there is a strong tendency to think of human beings as agents responsible for their own fates. This tendency is so pervasive that we even think of victims as responsible for their

[1] See, for example, *The Radical Therapist* II, Ballantine Books, N.Y., 1972.

misfortune (Lerner, 1965), and we perversely increase our blame of the
victim as the severity of his misfortune increases (Walster, 1966). Even
clearly accidental consequences are blamed on the victim because it
makes the world more predictable if we can say, "He deserved it," rather
than, "For some strange reason, it happened." Ironically, this is known
as the *theory of a just world.*

It is true that legal systems throughout history have been based on
the assumption that, at some point beyond certified idiocy, insanity,
nonintentionality, or extremity of circumstance (and we questioned
earlier the reliability of applying such labels), people are to be held responsible for their own actions. Perhaps Skinner's radical therapy of
assuming total environmental determinism is in part a reaction to the
just world theory which attributes every consequence to the person's
moral character and absolutely nothing to his or her circumstances.
Others, particularly those who take the Judeo-Christian view of man
seriously, will argue that the real state of the world is somewhere in between, that all our personal actions and life events reflect an interaction
of personal choice and effort, on the one hand, and the press of environment and circumstance, on the other. The disagreements come when
different individuals see the same event as the product of different
forces: The courtroom judge is relatively unsympathetic to the robber
who pleads that he had a mother who beat him. The robber's lawyer,
on the other hand, may invoke this explanation as a perfectly valid reason for lenient treatment or even perhaps total amnesty. Jeeves (1967)
maintains that such doublethink can even go on in the same person at
the same time, and by way of example points out that many clinical
psychologists, regardless of the school in which they were trained, talk
as if, up to the present, their clients' lives (and hence problems) have
been determined by circumstance, but that from this point on, the
client is a freely choosing agent of a rosier future. Fromm (1968) also
points out that had Marx totally believed his economic-determinist view
of history and had Freud totally espoused his own psychological determinism of personality, neither would have spearheaded movements
aimed at interrupting the very cycle of determinism that each postu-
lated. One might say the same of Skinner: No true missionary for
change can be a total determinist, and this is also suggested by the very
assertion of militant blacks, women, and others that one *can,* indeed,
rise above one's previous labels by insight, effort, and solidarity. Other-

wise, why bother trying, if choice and responsibility are totally illusory and if environmental contingencies determine all?

Unanswered Questions

How can we go about eliminating labels or their consequences? Evidence from studies of human learning suggest that this is a naive question. The essence of higher order learning is *concept formation,* and concept formation means categorizing and applying a name to the category. Are we supposed to put a moratorium on concept formation when it comes to learning about people? Evidence from sociology also suggests that "to believe that we can do away with the distinction between . . . *us* and *them* in social life is complete nonsense" (Hughes, 1962, pp. 8-9).

If social groupings with names attached are inevitable, what can be done about the often undesirable consequences of labels? This section will propose several possibilities that may seem utopian but which have their precedents.

Assuming Temporariness Instead of assuming permanence, could we think of the labels as describing temporary states which persons enter and leave at will? Some examples might help. One teacher in a Midwest college (whose social category under the old system of labels will remain a secret) often begins class by announcing which mood he is in for the day—these can range from a Jewish mood, a black mood, or a WASP mood, to any imaginable mood. Moods are thought of as temporary conditions which will pass so they might provide a useful rewording of the traditional group names. Speaking of "phases" also has possibilities, as when we speak of children going through a negative phase or a Daddy's-little-helper phase, both of which will pass. This language would allow boys and girls alike to go through a bullying phase, a dressing-up phase, a doll-playing phase, and any others which now are restricted to one sex or the other.

It is true that such temporariness makes the social world less predictable—we do not know what mood the teacher will be in tomorrow, nor do we know whether this little boy will act the way little boys are traditionally *supposed* to act. In actuality, however, our current predictions are not really predictions in the scientific sense but just self-fulfilling prophecies.

This way of thinking would allow whites to go through black moods or phases and vice versa; it would permit men to stay home with the children in a motherly phase while women could work as foremen, in a boss phase. Note, this system does not eliminate the old terms—it still assumes that *motherly* means taking care of children. Replacing the old terms with new ones may follow if it turns out that more men than women are in a motherly mood in 1976, for instance. Even if the old vocabulary remains, however, it does not pose the same problems, for one would not *be* a mother, one would just *be in* that type of mood, and anyone could do it.

Shifting Symbolic Power Simply adding the term *mood* or *phase* to the old category names is not enough, however. The definition of their content is still problematic. The solution may seem simple: if being motherly is bad, no one will want to be motherly and the category will disappear. Suppose, however, someone wants to be motherly for a while, or just finds him- or herself in a motherly mood, and resents the negative overtones. It would seem clear that the power to define the features of the category-mood-phase should lie with those inside, instead of those outside, the group. Something akin to this happened with the Black-Is-Beautiful movement. Traditionally, Anglo-Saxon skin, hair styles, dress, and speech were considered the models of excellence, and anything different (including Afro-American skin, hair styles, dress and speech) was less than perfect. Why should an outside group dictate the definitions for persons in an Afro mood?

Somehow the power shifted, and the redefinitions were so successful that they spilled over into traditional white society. White college students have worn African *Dashikis,* and with permanents or natural curl have worn their hair in Afro styles. They should not be denied the possibility of entering this mood; nor should all persons currently considered black be forced into it. But it should be agreed that those who do enter have the right to define the features themselves.

This makes the process sound terribly rational, while power struggles, symbolic or otherwise, do not generally take place at such a conference-table level. How, then, did the Afro movement succeed in gaining its power to define the situation? No one has adequately answered this. It is a question worth pursuing for anyone interested in liberating persons from inherited and imposed definitions.

Implications for Society

Substituting the temporary moodlike notion of groups for the current permanent-labels notion cannot be legislated nor will it happen by wishing it. One way it may occur is through extended games or role-playing exercises.

Children have always had their games, playing at being cops and robbers, cowboys and Indians, mother and father, doctor and patient, and so on. That, in fact, is how they learned to *become* cops or robbers, mothers or fathers, and so on. By the time they reach adulthood, they no longer have the option to try on different roles, except in theaters, on an acknowledged stage. What some new commercial games permit, indeed require, is such a temporary changing of roles.

What do these games or exercises for adults look like? At the level of parlor games, some commercial role-switching exercises already exist: *Black and White* is one, *Man and Woman* another. The rules of *Black and White* enable "black" players to collect welfare payments and require "white" players to go bankrupt instead. They permit whites to have all the other economic advantages, however, like a loaded game of monopoly.

At a less make-believe level, it is not impossible to imagine temporary role switching, for we can even find precedents around us. Several traditional societies have a *couvade* which has men playing the role of their pregnant wives and experiencing labor pains as the child is about to be born (Burton & Whiting, 1961). The United States has its leap year which makes it legitimate for girls to chase their boyfriends. And some schools have a special day when students play teacher and vice versa.

This proposal, then, is not different from what already exists in some times and some places. It is, rather, a recommendation that we extend the areas in which such role switching, or mood changing, may occur.

Having reached this conclusion, the authors should really go back to the beginning of this chapter and put quotation marks around all the group labels employed—the word *white* should never appear without quotation marks, nor should *woman, black, Chicano,* and any of the other terms traditionally used to categorize people. But the authors are in a tired mood, the publishers might be in an angry mood, and the printers might be in an "oh-come-on-now" mood. So it is left to the reader to put quotes around these terms in his own mind, at least, and to liberate us all from our labels.

Chapter 5

Liberation: Countercultures and Revolution

PROPOSITION

It is not only the labels attached to people that produce self-fulfilling prophecies about their status, roles, or abilities. The rewards and punishments (positive and negative reinforcers) attached to the behaviors assumed to be appropriate for a given group will help to perpetuate that behavior. Often such behavior becomes so persistent and predictable within group members that it is assumed to be the reflection of innate, unchangeable personality traits. Much countercultural and revolutionary activity is concerned with redefining so-called innate group-traits as traits which have really been *reinforced* into continued existence by more powerful majority groups. Changes in the social environment brought about actively or coincidentally facilitate the process of self-redefinition within minority groups, as does the example of other revolutionary groups. Ways of reacting to changed self-definition include individual assimilation, group separatism, and demands for greater control of resources.

Illustrative Work

For many of us—the unpoor, the unblack, the ungay, the unred, the un-
female—what knowledge we have of liberation movements may consist
of a number of unclear generalizations, a few slogans, and certain apparently dramatic incidents covered all too well by the media. A group of
Indians take possession of Alcatraz Island. Homophiles in New York
wreck a syndicate-dominated bar in a spontaneous revolt against the
protection racket. A group of women protest the holding of an antiwar
fund-raising dinner in the mansion of *Playboy* magnate Hugh Hefner.
An improbable alliance arises in Chicago between ghetto blacks and
poor white migrants from Appalachia.

The dynamics of these movements and their activities can be very
difficult to trace if one is not a member of such a group. Their literature
has been to a large extent ephemeral, consisting of privately circulated
pamphlets, statements, papers, and newsletters that rarely find their
way to the periodicals room of the local library. Often the particular
movement rhetoric may seem vague, oratorical, and stereotyped to persons outside the cause; and members of the press, which is often viewed
as simply another tool in the service of the Establishment, are regarded
with a suspicion that makes accurate coverage difficult even when the
reporter feels sympathy for the cause.

We do not claim to be able to present an analysis of all aspects of
current liberation movements—such an assumption would certainly con-
stitute a very naive arrogance. There are, however, concepts and studies
in the broad social-psychological tradition which may help to synthe-
size the sometimes dizzying scope of movement activities and writings.
In this chapter, we shall be using some of these approaches, as well as
letting the movements speak for themselves.

The Minority Group Personality: Innate or Acquired? *Personality*
has been variously defined in the psychological literature. Allport calls
it "the dynamic organization within the individual of those psychophys-
ical systems that determine his characteristic behavior and thought"
(1961, p. 28). Guilford speaks of "a person's unique pattern of traits"
(1959, p. 5), and McClelland refers to personality as "the most adequate
conceptualization of a person's behavior in all its detail" (1951, p. 69).
While at first glance these definitions might seem rather different from

one another, they do have certain assumptions in common. Words like organization, system, characteristic, and pattern imply that there is a measure of consistency or permanence to one's personality. Terms like unique and individual suggest also that no two of us are exactly alike.

Researchers in this area study the impact of experience on personality and the possible meaning of differences among individuals, as well as investigating so-called abnormal behavior and personality in the therapy setting. To a major degree, however, research and writing has focused primarily on the individual per se and his or her personal history, with only secondary reference to the family history, and with even less emphasis given to the influence of the wider social setting as a determinant of personality traits. Even when scholars have studied, for example, the Negro personality or the female personality, they have rarely gone beyond a mere description of existing traits to speculate about the possible social origins of their characterologies. Thus it may be shown that blacks have a higher than average incidence of paranoia than whites (Pettigrew, 1964, chap. 4), and that women have lower self-esteem and less self-confidence than men (Terman and Tyler, 1954). But much less has been said of the possible social pressure which may have been a major source of such characteristics. Recently, a number of writers from liberation causes have taken exception to the narrowness of such an approach with its implications that certain group-prevalent traits are internally stable and relatively unalterable, rather than adaptive responses to a basically hostile environment. Thus, Sidney Abbot and Barbara Love, in writing about the lesbian experience in America say:

> The emotional development that enables a lesbian to throw off the sex roles and sex restrictions universally accepted by our society has been commonly described as a psychopathology: a mental sickness. It is assumed that something in the individual's family environment has caused the child's development to take a wrong turn. However, some progressive psychiatrists and social workers have begun to talk about a concept called sociopathology: a sickness in society. They have found that the individuals they have treated for so-called personal problems have real problems which they are in no position to control. The environment threatens them, even physically. This continual state of threat leads to tension, which leads to various emotional problems which cannot be solved by treatment because they are perpetuated by real pressure from a hostile society. The con-

cept of sociopathology fosters a need for systematic analysis of all women's behavior and sheds particular light on this society's rigidity and unwillingness to tolerate many life-styles for women. It points to external reasons for lesbian's distress and emotional problems. The problems of lesbians—guilt, fear, and self-hatred—can therefore be regarded as a part of a sociopathology, part of what is wrong with our society, preventing whole categories of people from being happy and productive (Gornick and Moran, 1971, p. 440).

And in a similar vein, Frantz Fanon, the black Antillean psychiatrist who has written biting indictments of the effects of racism, writes:

My patient is suffering from an inferiority complex. His psychic structure is in danger of deterioration. . . . If he is overwhelmed to such a degree by the wish to be white, it is because he lives in a society that makes his inferiority complex possible, in a society that proclaims the superiority of one race; to the identical degree to which that society creates difficulties for him, he will find himself thrust into a neurotic situation. What emerges then is the need for combined action on the individual and the group. As a psychiatrist I should help my patient to become conscious of his unconscious, and to abandon his attempts at hallucinatory whitening, but also act in the direction of a change in the social structure (1952, p. 100).

Low Social Status as a Determinant of Personality   Among personality theorists, a notable exception to the tendency to ignore the impact of wider social influences was Gordon Allport, who wrote at length in *The Nature of Prejudice* (1954) about "Traits Due to Victimization." Writing primarily about blacks and Jews, Allport included the following personality characteristics as possible outcomes of victimization by the society at large: sensitivity, submission, fantasies of power, desire for protection, indirectness, ingratiation (that is, flattering and pandering to the ego of a more powerful individual), petty revenge and sabotage, sympathy, self-hatred of one's own group alternating with self- and group-aggrandizement, display of flashy status symbols, compassion for the underprivileged, identification with the dominant group's norms, and passivity (chap. 9).

Almost twenty years later, with the renewing of women's consciousness regarding their own victimization, Freeman (1971) pointed out some intriguing parallels between Allport's characterization of Jews and blacks and the personality profile of young girls drawn up by Terman and Tyler (1954) based on a review of the then existing literature on sex differences in young children. These two researchers found that girls are typified by sensitivity, conformity to social pressures, responsiveness to the environment, ease of social control, ingratiation, sympathy, low levels of aspiration, compassion for the underprivileged, and anxiety. In comparison to boys, they were more nervous, unstable, neurotic, socially dependent, and submissive. They had less self-confidence, lower opinions of themselves and of girls in general (as compared to their opinions of boys), and were more timid, nurturant, fearful, and passive. Girls' opinions of themselves and their own abilities grew progressively worse with age, while their opinions of boys' abilities grew better and better despite the fact that girls do consistently better than boys academically until well into high school. Boys did not show a similar tendency to feelings of inferiority: their self-esteem increased with age, and their opinion of girls' abilities grew worse.

Freeman's line of argument implies, in effect, that in *any* group (be it women, blacks, American Indians, or whatever) whose survival depends on the good will of a more powerful group, there will develop the necessary traits to ensure that survival: for example, if you are black or female, you are traditionally not supposed to take the initiative in an interaction with a white male. Therefore, since you are not supposed to find out by direct inquiry what is in the mind of this more powerful other, you will understandably learn to be very sensitive to that person's nonverbal reactions. Your survival might very well depend on interpreting correctly the real meaning of a raised eyebrow and acting accordingly—hence the so-called greater intuitiveness, sensitivity, and indirectness of both blacks and women. Similarly, the traits of ingratiation, submission, and conformity would be interpreted not as inherent traits that would inevitably appear in all blacks (or women, or Indians) at all times, but as sensible strategies for dealing with more powerful authorities in whose hands one's fate may ultimately lie. To be an uppity nigger or an aggressive woman (that is, to attempt independent action and achievement) may result in social disapproval and ostracism at the very least and, not infrequently, in actual physical harm at the hands of the dominant group. Lynchings of blacks on the flimsiest of pretexts and the burning of so-called witches in the past may be seen as an affirmation of the optimal survival strategy of the underdog: be un-obtrusive; avoid at all costs offending the more powerful other, assure him of his superiority; and learn to read his moods. In the language of the behaviorists, forthrightness, initiative, and independent achievement disappear from these oppressed groups because these traits are punished (Pascale & Kidder, 1973). The opposite behaviors, so aptly summarized by Allport, persist because they are rewarded, or positively reinforced— or at least because they are less apt to lead to punishment.

Raised Status as an Explanation of Changed Personality   If this ex-planation has any validity, then there is a relatively easy way to test it out: What happens to the so-called typical characteristics of minority-group members when, by accident or design, they are placed in atypical settings which reinforce new and very different behaviors?

On a Six Nations Indian Reserve in Canada, there is a totally Indian-staffed school system whose rate of student graduation from high school has, for several years, exceeded the Canadian national average—in direct contradiction to the stereotype of the shiftless, lazy Indian who is in-capable of making much use of higher formal education. How has this come about? The superintendent of this school system, himself Indian, maintains that it is due to the fact that all the teachers, besides being well trained academically, have a strong sense of their own "Indianness.' Culturally and linguistically, they can relate to the school children in terms that they understand, and at the same time provide visible evi-dence that one can "make it" on the white man's terms without neces-sarily becoming a "White Indian." They are able to reinforce a confi-dent self-image in children who, under white teachers who regarded them as less educable, might well come to believe in this assumption of infer-iority. "When you've got your head up in the air," comments superin-tendent Hill, "you can see where you're going" (Hill, 1970). In an environment where competent performance and confident self-image are reinforced, these Indian children show themselves very capable academically.

Shortly after the Israeli victory in the Six-Day Middle East war in 1967, a particular poster became quite popular among young American-Jewish people: it showed what was meant to be a short, bearded, be-spectacled Jewish gentleman with a pleased grin on his face changing into a Superman costume in a telephone booth. The message was very clear: Surprise, surprise! We *aren't* soft, flabby, apologetic whipping-boys. We have shown that we can defend ourselves, so don't be deceived by appearances. Around this same time, the militant Jewish Defense League evolved as a vehicle for the protection of urban Jews by organized patrolling of those areas of the city where Jews had been most frequently harassed. The JDL also gives training in the martial arts, such as karate and aki-do, and stresses the necessity of reversing traditional stereotypes concerning Jews by adopting and reinforcing an attitude of militant preparedness. Here again, it can be seen that when people's stereotyped expectations of a given group are somehow contradicted by a salient, forceful event, members of that group may also begin to act in a way which contradicts the stereotype.

A third example of the impact of changed environment on so-called typical minority-group characteristics comes from a field experiment in which the deliberate manipulation of a recreation program curriculum was shown to have measurable positive effects on the self-esteem of two groups of black children as they came into a summer recreation program in Evanston, Illinois, using a variation of the Clarks' "doll-preference" technique (Clark & Clark, 1950). Children were asked to rank-order from most- to least-liked a series of four pictures: a white boy, a white girl, a black boy, and a black girl. Typically, at the beginning of the recreation program, the black boys' rank order of preference for the four pictures was: white boy, black boy, white girl, black girl, and the black girls' rank order tended to be: white girl, black girl, white boy, black boy. Of the two groups participating in the recreation program, one then had a standard recreation program curriculum of swimming, sports, crafts, outings, stories, and films. The second group had similar activities—but these activities were black-enriched. That is, the films and library books for this group were deliberately chosen for Afro-American content. When an outing was made to a local fire station, it was arranged that a black fireman be the guide, and so forth. At the end of the recreation program, when each child was again asked to rank-order the four child-pictures, the children of the standard curriculum tended to stick to the same rank-order as they had at the first of the program, but the children of the black-enriched group showed a significant shift in their choices: both sexes now tended to choose the black boy before the white boy and the black girl before the white girl. It would seem that even a month spent in an environment where blacks feature prominently and positively was enough to reduce the children's previously low regard for themselves and for other black children.

Reactions to Changed Self-Definition

Individual Assimilation to the Dominant Norm Various writers (Pettigrew, 1964; Baughman, 1971) have pointed out that even *before* the changing social context facilitated self-redefinition, minority group members have often known that they had more abilities than the dominant group gave them credit for, even while realizing that open assertion of those abilities would be unwise. Thomas Pettigrew, a social psychologist concerned with racism and its impact on black Americans, points out that one possible reaction to minority status is that of *moving towards the oppressor*—that is, seeking individual acceptance into an integrated society of the sort which has traditionally only been available to the dominant group. Alice Rossi, a feminist sociologist (1969), calls similar strivings among women part of the *assimilationist* model of equality, which asserts that women should seek their place with men in the political and occupational world in sufficient numbers to show, eventually, a roughly equal distribution of the sexes in all the high-status, high-paying positions of society. Black organizations such as the National Association for the Advancement of Coloured People and the Congress on Racial Equality typify this desire for a fairer share of the existing resources, or a bigger slice of the pie. The National Organization of Women and the Jewish B'nai B'rith Hillel Organization espouse similar aims for their particular constituencies.

The assimilationist model of equality is seen by many other levels of liberation struggles as essentially an individual solution, a solution which advocates for the most part adhering to the dominant group's norms and asks only for the chance to be allowed the normal fruits of such diligence. On the individual level, this may have some not-too-surprising consequences. Even if the accomplished minority group member "makes it" in middle-class society, it is still the dominant group which calls the shots. It is they who set the standards—of work, of fashion, of recreation. The result can be what Pettigrew calls "dissociation" (1964, chap. 9)—being one's real self outside the work setting, but a necessarily very different person in it. Grier and Cobbs (1968) cite the instance of a black businessman who, despite his financial success, had a personal manner of extreme deference, never raising his voice, always understating his case, his gestures measured and "noninflammatory." Grier and Cobbs speculate on the conflict that must take place inside such persons:

> Starting with slavery . . . black men have had to devise ways of expressing themselves uniquely and individually and in a manner that was not threatening to the white man. . . . It would be easy to write off this man as an isolated, passive individual, but his whole community looks upon his career as a success story. He made it in a system to a position of influence and means. And it took an aggressive, driving, determined man to make it against the odds he faced. We must ask how much energy is required for him to conceal his drive so thoroughly. And we wonder what would happen if his controls ever failed (p. 67).

Bird (1968) has found that women in high places face a similar conflict: The individual talent and determination which got them where they are must often be scrupulously hidden before male colleagues if work is to proceed smoothly. She reports that women in executive positions often try to ward off hostility by phrasing their orders as suggestions and planting ideas in the heads of their male colleagues in the hope that they will perceive them as their own. A successful woman sociologist has commented that she always feels apprehensive when giving a paper unless she periodically interjects humorous asides. By making the listeners laugh, she feels that this defuses, at least in part, the hostility they may feel towards a woman in a position of such obvious authority (Bart, 1971).

Homophiles of both sexes have traditionally had to not just minimize, but fully disguise their true natures in order to get ahead at all in the predominantly "straight" world:

> Homosexuals tended to be isolated and inhibited, having taken the one course they could really afford, which was to pass for heterosexual in order to pursue careers and life within the society, both of which would likely be destroyed were their homosexuality exposed. So their endeavor was not to battle the dragon, but to sneak around it, to "get by," with a minimum of pain (Lessard, 1970).

It is not difficult to see that a lot of anxiety may be generated by the necessity of "walking on eggs" (as one woman executive put it) in the presence of persons from the dominant majority. Pugh (1943) found that black students attending integrated high schools had a higher level of anxiety than both their white classmates and their black peers attending nonintegrated schools. Maccoby (1963) and Horner (1971) have observed that women in general, but particularly those who are highly achievement-oriented, show more anxiety in test situations than males. While a certain degree of anxiety is an asset to productive thinking, high or sustained levels of it can be counterproductive and debilitating. One might predict the same difficulties for the loophole black man, or the white Indian or the black Englishman of the colonial period in Africa.

Such assimilation, or moving towards the oppressor, is seen by most militant liberation groups as a preliberation or even counterrevolutionary solution. It may materially benefit isolated individuals (although, as we have just seen, possibly at tremendous psychic cost to themselves), but it does not substantially improve the lot of the oppressed group as a whole, nor does it seem to reduce the stereotypes held by the dominant group concerning the less powerful minority: the "honest Indian," the "smart Nigger," and the "woman who thinks like a man" are, by the very existence of such phrases, deemed exceptions which prove the general rule. Further, the assimilating person is often expected to achieve twice as much to get half as far, and not only do that in relative isolation, but often with the very real fear of being replaced or passed over when it comes to job advancement. This is not to say that the assimilationist solution is necessarily a right or wrong one for any given individual, but merely that it has in recent years been seen as inadequate to the needs of many, if not most, of the oppressed-group membership. Nonetheless, when an organized, more broadly based struggle does evolve, it is often these very persons, the ones who have managed to succeed in the dominant culture, who, having relevant skills and information, find themselves, often reluctantly, in key leadership posts in the struggle. How such struggles may evolve is the topic with which we will next concern ourselves.

Movements As More-Than-Individual Solutions: How Are They Born? It would seem that there are three separate things which, singly or together, contribute to the formation of a liberation struggle: first, a general social context and spirit of the times which is somehow relevant to that particular struggle: second, a particularly salient event, or "happening" which focuses on and unites (often without forethought) the group; third, the existence of one or more similar group struggles which can be used, in some ways, as a role model.

The Social Context It would be difficult to imagine a wide-ranging women's movement in the absence of reliable contraceptive technology. A woman who has no reliable method of birth control other than abstinence is, if she is involved in a continuing relationship with a man, never free until menopause from the risk of unplanned pregnancy. When this is the case, women *are* less mobile and more prone to being incapacitated at unpredictable intervals (although many in the women's movement claim that the degree of incapacitation has always been exaggerated and taken advantage of by the power structure). Similarly, it would be difficult to imagine a strong, enduring women's movement in an environment where all heavy labor had to be accomplished with human strength alone. Where the strength differential between men and women matters, as it did in preindustrial, nonmechanized societies, women will certainly be harder pressed to formulate a case for diversifying their own roles. Technology has helped set the scene for the women's movement in yet another way: in times past, without the medical sophistication we now enjoy, the rate of infant mortality was so high that, to keep the population even stable, a high birthrate was necessary. To ensure that even two of your children reached adulthood, you would have to conceive a great many more than just two. In addition, in a predominantly rural, nontechnologized economy, children are economic wealth: the larger the family, the more land that can be farmed; and hence childbearing, far from being mere ego gratification, was directly related to the acquisition of wealth. All this has changed greatly in recent times. Large families, far from being economic assets in a largely urban society, must be valued for personal satisfaction reasons alone. Concern over a geometrically expanding world population has reduced even the social prestige of large families. Jobs solely reliant on muscular strength are steadily disappearing, and birth control is becoming steadily more reliable. These factors, while perhaps not the only ones which contributed to the emergence of the women's movement in the mid-sixties, would seem to be indispensable to it.

With regard to the emergence of a black liberation movement, one can again cite relevant features of the social context of the sixties. In the first place, it was during this decade that one African state after another achieved independence from white colonial rule. Today, few remaining enclaves of white supremacy are concentrated around the southern end of the African continent, and even these feel far from secure about the continuation of white rule. Black Panther ideologist Eldridge Cleaver commented:

> If the nations of Asia, Latin America, and Africa are strong and free, the black man in America will be safe and secure and free to live in dignity and self-respect. It is a cold fact that while the nations of Africa, Asia, and Latin America were shackled in colonial bondage, the black American was held tightly in the vise of oppression and not permitted to utter a sound of protest; but when these nations started bidding for their freedom . . . it was then that the white man yielded what he did—out of sheer necessity (1968, pp. 125–127).

Cleaver also states that a disproportionate number of black men were sent to Vietnam due to the inability of men with lower education to get the same military exemptions as college students. Those who returned (complete with all the skills necessary to carry on a revolution) were all too often unable to get the jobs claimed to be so universally available to ex-servicemen, thus setting into motion what we have called elsewhere in this book the *revolution of rising expectations*. It is not the totally downtrodden who are most prone to violence against the system, but rather those who have begun to experience some improvement and measured the gap that still remains.

So the tenor of the times and larger social and economic issues do make a difference. This is the soil bed in which liberation movements grow. But given the appropriate social conditions for this kind of movement to grow, is there then a triggering mechanism? a spark that lights the accumulated fuel and tinder? a straw that breaks the camel's back? It appears that this, too, is often the case.

Happenings that Become Causes   A strange thing happened in Watts in 1965, August. The blacks, who in this land of private property have all private and no property, got excited into a uproar because they noticed a cop before he had a chance to wash the blood off his hands. Usually the police department can handle such flare-ups. But this time it was different. Things got out of hand. The blacks were running amok, burning, shooting, breaking. The police department was powerless to control them. . . . Out came the National Guard, that ambiguous hybrid from the twilight zone where the domestic army merges with the international. Unleashing their for-midable firepower, they crushed the blacks. But things will never be the same again. Too many people saw that those who turned the other cheek in Watts got their whole head blown off (Cleaver, 1968, pp. 131–132).

Cleaver clearly saw the Watts riot as a watershed in the black move-ment—an event of unprecedented, unpredictable unit whose occurrence escalated the black struggle to a new level of militance. But other levels preceded this one, and they too were often marked by an event which became a rallying cry. A poll conducted in 1963 found that two-thirds of all blacks interviewed saw the 1954 Supreme Court school desegre-gation decision as being just such an event: "It started the ball rolling," commented one respondent. "It gave us the heart to fight," said another (Pettigrew, 1964, p. 10). Again in 1955, in Montgomery, Alabama, Rosa Parks, by the simple act of refusing to give her bus seat to a white man, unwittingly committed the right symbolic act at just the right time to spark the Montgomery bus boycott and a subsequent decade of civil rights demonstrations. It would seem that such events, each significantly less polite and moderate than its predecessors, helped to catalyze a dif-fuse spirit of dissatisfaction into progressively more organized and less compromising protest.

The more recently born gay liberation movement also looks to a particular event in time and space as the significant happening which started bringing homophiles all over the country "out of the closets and into the streets." One reporter describes the effect of the Christopher Street Riot as follows:

The movement was born one night in August, 1969, when the New York police raided the Stonewall Inn, a gay bar on Christopher Street. It was by no means the first time—few of the many gay bars in the Village vicinity were immune to the arbitrary raids which usually ended in several arrests and many more bruises and broken heads. But this time, to the amazement of the Sixth Precinct, the homosexuals refused to take their punishment. The sissies fought back. Word of the brawl travelled, the gay community turned out in force, and the battle spread from the bar into what became known as the Christopher Street riot, a free-for-all in which cars were over-turned, fires lit, and police sent to hospital. After that, the image of the homosexual in the eyes of the world, and, more important, in his own eyes as well, was irrevocably altered (Lessard, 1970, p. 40).

By the time an anniversary march of gay persons was organized in New York City a year later to commemorate the Christopher Street riot, the Gay Liberation Front was an international movement, complete with offices, newspapers, speakers' bureaus, and rallying slogans.

While by themselves such events would probably not create the unity necessary for an organized movement, we have seen that they can act as catalysts, increasing the tempo of an already developing dissatis-faction and providing an often unplanned taste of what can be accomplished by united action.

"If They Can Do It, So Can We" A third factor which may aid in the formation of a movement is simply the impact of seeing others do it. The importance of such *role modeling* in getting persons to try out new responses which they have never practiced before is a well-demon-strated tenet of social learning theory (Bandura & Walters, 1963). These researchers have shown in their laboratory experiments that a person is more likely to imitate a model who is perceived as similar to herself or himself than one who is perceived as dissimilar. Thus, it is hardly sur-prising that, once the black movement started to gain momentum, other nonwhite, low-status groups should begin to consider similar possibilities for themselves. Chicanos, Puerto Ricans, and American Indians took heart as they saw black Americans openly defying the myths of what Cleaver called the white "Omnipotent Administrator" and the black "Supermasculine Menial." This same aspect of social learning theory may also explain why, despite a proliferation of strikes and community organizations among Mexican-American farm laborers from 1900 on, only in the mid-sixties did *La Causa* really become a nationwide, viable rallying cry. Until the outbreak of the 1965 grapeyards strike, farm-labor organizations, while they spoke on behalf of Chicanos, were made

up almost entirely of Anglos. Only when Cesar Chavez came forward with his National Farm Workers Association did *La Huelga* bloom into *La Causa:* the movement was finally being directed by people of its own constituency (Howard, 1970).

It has also been said that the black struggle in many ways provided a model for the women's movement, and women in the movement have often compared their castelike, ascribed status to that of blacks—a parallel which has been written about by perceptive sociologists but largely ignored, long before either blacks or women really mobilized (Myrdal, 1944; Hacker, 1951). Gay liberation acknowledges the example of the women's movement as the two work among their respective populations to gain a greater flexibility of definition for sex roles.

Social learning theory also points out that, while the existence of a salient model may get the new behavior going, it will only last if it is reinforced. Hence the success of first confrontations may be a crucial variable in keeping the ball rolling. Even the intermittent winning of small concessions thereafter, provided there is not active, large-scale repressiveness which outweighs such victories, may be sufficient reinforcement to ensure the momentum of the movement.

Having come together, what then is the course of the embryonic movement? We do these movements a grave injustice if we simply try to force the dynamics of all of them into a single model. Each has its own unique concerns and strategies which reflect that group's cultural history and predominant environment. Nevertheless, there do seem to be some common denominators, and we have chosen to discuss these in terms of two distinct yet overlapping functions: those of internal consciousness raising and external action. These two functions can and usually do take place concurrently, although there is a distinct tendency for the particular type of activism at any given time to reflect the results of consciousness raising. For this reason, we will deal with the latter concept first.

Movement Activity: Separation and Consciousness Raising In Pettigrew's (1964) discussion of ways in which oppressed groups deal with their oppression, he includes the option of "moving away from the oppressor," or simply separating oneself psychologically (and sometimes even physically) from interaction with the dominant group wherever possible. Such separatism would seem to be a prominent feature of

almost all liberation struggles. There may be differences both within
and between movement groups regarding how much, and for how long,
the group should separate itself from the dominant culture, but nonetheless, many members of such groups find themselves, at least for a
time, cloistering themselves—totally or intermittently—for the purpose
of "getting it together."

There are some very obvious reasons for doing this. If, as Allport
says, one of the traits due to victimization is a tendency to defer to
members of the dominant group, it is unlikely that one will reverse such
a long-conditioned tendency while still mingling with that dominant
group. The rationale for excluding men from women's liberation groups
centers around precisely this danger: Women have been socialized to defer to men in discussions, to tolerate interruptions from them, and to
direct their remarks to them for endorsement. Men, by the same token,
claim those in the women's movement, assume that they can interrupt,
dominate discussions, and manipulate women by the reward of attention or the threat of withdrawing it (Henley, 1970). For women to be
able to practice being assertive, articulate, and focused on each other
(rather than on the hope of *male* approval) requires, for a time, a totally
male-free environment. Many women's groups have devoted considerable
effort to creating a discussion atmosphere which encourages the more
timid to express their opinions and feelings, and hierarchy is minimized,
often by drawing lots to determine tasks. Agendas may be determined
by circulating a clipboard among members at the beginning of meetings.
During meetings, members may be required to adhere to a "speakers'
list"—that is, rather than spontaneously interjecting comments into an
ongoing report, a hand is raised, the name of the would-be speaker noted
by the chairperson, and that person speaks only after all those preceding
her on the speakers' list have had their say. What such a procedure loses
in spontaneity, it gains in providing an atmosphere in which the shyer
members can begin to practice their speaking skills free from the risk of
being "outarticulated" by the more practiced and assertive members of
the group.

Separation also allows concentration: concentration on researching
and setting down (perhaps for the first time) the common history of the
group as seen not by historians of the dominant culture but by the group
itself; concentration on evolving a working theory of what the group is,
and wants, since it is soon realized that random activism without such a

theory to unify it will gain little of permanence for the group as a whole; and concentration on evolving cultural expressions unique to that group and not subject to the standards of the dominant majority—in art, literature, journalism, and poetry. Within most liberation movements, there can be found vehicles for this sort of expression: newspapers, magazines, journals for poetry, prose, and graphics, artists' collectives devoted to the portrayal of the group's *ethos,* and informal schools offering courses which help integrate potential recruits into the movement.

Separation also allows for the independent development of skills normally available only to members of the dominant group. Seldom has a woman, a black man, a Chicano or a Puerto Rican run an aboveground newspaper or even a small office. Almost all have been at the labor rather than the management end of the work continuum. By being able to practice management skills, even on a small scale, and evolve unique ways of running things free from the supervision of persons from the dominant culture (even well-meaning liberals can make the mistake of showing movement members "how to run" their own liberation struggle), members of the movement may attain both the experience and the confidence to challenge the dominant culture using not only its own methods, but new ones as well.

External activism does not usually wait until the need for internal consciousness raising has been fully satisfied—indeed, the two functions tend to alternate or take place concurrently. But as consciousness of self and group aims crystallizes, actions in the world at large become more specific and more unified. Let us now turn our attention to the nature of such activism.

Movement Activism: Demanding Control of Resources As was pointed out earlier, it is no longer seen by many as enough to insist on a bigger slice of the existing social pie—although this may be an interim goal at some stage, and indeed may be seen as quite adequate to those of a merely reformist bent or gradualist philosophy. To more and more persons involved in liberation movements, true liberation cannot come about until the very relevance of existing institutions is pointedly questioned. It is seen as a paradox by some that, after a decade of struggling for school integration, the most insistent black voices now call for *separate* schools for blacks. The difference, of course, is that to separate would now be a *freely chosen* option, and that such schools would be controlled and staffed by the black community: "We don't need the white man in the schools teaching us how to be black. . . We want black teachers and black principals deciding the education process of the black person" (Cleaver, 1969). Thus, as such groups begin to move in an organized fashion "against the oppressor" (Pettigrew's third "reaction to oppression"), demands which once focused largely on a right to equal access to *existing* resources now shift to demands *for resources to be used as that group sees fit.* Thus, in 1967, Canada's Native Alliance for Red Power was demanding that the existing federal Indian Affairs Branch be "under the control of and staffed by Indians up to and including a minister of the Crown, and these representatives be elected and responsible to the Indians of Canada" (Jack, 1970). But three years later, the very existence of the Branch as an institution relevant to the needs of Indians had come into question: Indian people could fill the ranks of the bureaucracy but still become corrupted and coopted. They would have to share the views of the existing white bureaucrats before even being taken on as civil servants. They would have to become "white Indians." And so, in 1970, it was concluded that "gaining power in our reservations and communities, and power over our lives, will entail the abolition of the Indian Act, and the destruction of the colonial office—the Indian Affairs Branch. . . . To us, Red Power means the gathering together of *Indian* people to solve their problems, whether political, social, or economical" (Jack, 1970). By the same token, radical women insist that it is not enough to have day care centers run by industries for their employees if they simply create in the working mother a greater obligation to accept whatever other working conditions exist in that industry. They are firm in their insistence that whatever forms of day care evolve, and however they are financed, control of policy and resources would be in the hands of those who use them, not those who happened to agree to—and even underwrite—their existence. There is a strong feeling among all liberation struggles that "freedom" also means the freedom to form *new* institutions based on the particular group's need, and not merely an invitation to proportional representation and a voice in the institutions established by the majority culture.

Unanswered Questions

A young black women professor recounts the following anecdote:

> Years ago I did a terrible thing. I edited a copy of a young male
> student's paper, "Reflections on Black Women," so that all refer-
> ences to "male" and "female" were changed to "us" and "them."
> After several months elapsed, I read the paper during one of our
> after-class beer chats. And sure enough everyone . . . agreed it was
> the usual racist shit. As a matter of fact, the author of the original
> piece was even more vitriolic in his condemnation of the bigotry
> and hypocrisy than anyone else. Of course, he went into a tirade
> about my ethics when I announced that the paper, his paper, origi-
> nally was not about Black and White but about Men and Women.
> But after the smoke cleared, we all sat and talked for hours, sharing
> such painfully private experiences, such poignant struggles with the
> rubber stamp of what a girl's supposed to be like, and what a boy's
> supposed to be like, that attendance in the class dropped off drasti-
> cally and we found it difficult to face each other for weeks. But at
> least the point had been made: racism and male chauvinism are anti-
> people. And a man cannot be politically correct and a chauvinist
> too (Cade, 1970).

It is possible that there is evolving a common realization among
movements that, indeed, even the oppressed themselves cannot be "politically correct" and still participate, pecking-order fashion, in the oppression of other out-groups. Thus white women must reexamine their
own racism, and black men their male chauvinism. Mothers must ponder
how they unconsciously exert arbitrary authority over children, and
"straight" blacks how they automatically tend to hold the gay world in
contempt. Thus, Huey Newton, in his office as Minister of Defense for
the Black Panther Party, ultimately came to write and circulate some
very trenchant comments on the necessity for revolutionary solidarity
among blacks, women, and homosexuals:

> Whatever your personal opinions and your insecurities are about . . .
> the various liberation movements among homosexuals and women,
> we should try to unite with them in a revolutionary fashion. I say
> "whatever your insecurities are" because, as we very well know,
> sometimes our first instinct is to want to hit a homosexual in the
> mouth and tell a woman to be quiet. . . . Remember, we haven't es-

tablished a revolutionary value system; we're only in the process of establishing it. I don't remember us ever constituting any value that said that a revolutionary should say offensive things towards homosexuals, or that a revolutionary should make sure that women do not speak out about their own particular kind of oppression. . . . The women's liberation front and gay liberation front are our friends, they are potential allies, and we need as many allies as possible" (Newton, 1970).

It is still an open question as to whether the unity among liberation movements idealized by Huey Newton can become a solid, ongoing reality. Once each movement has begun to press for its own particular demands from the existing power structure, will it in fact be possible to forge such an organized metastruggle? Many feel that this is possible even, or perhaps especially, in the economically tight years of the early seventies. The continued frustration of rising expectations developed in the prosperous sixties may combine with the realization on the part of more and more young people that ordinary, garden-variety diligence can no longer guarantee even a white middle-class male a place in the sun during these years of rising professional unemployment. What, then, would they lose by joining forces with those already committed to the realization—at whatever cost—of a more equitable society? Nothing at all, would reply the committed radicals of these various struggles: You have nothing to lose but your chains!

Implications for Society

The end result of such an attitude represents yet another step away from the assimilationist ethic. To borrow a phrase from Rossi (1969), it ultimately calls for more of a *hybrid* model of equality, which would require a basic restructuring of all existing institutions in order to ensure that the individual human needs of *all* sectors of the population are met—not just for physical well-being, but for creativity and fellowship as well. Whether such a restructuring can take place quickly enough or thoroughly enough without a total societal revolution is a question usually answered *Yes* by optimistic reformists but resoundingly *No* by those who compose the core of liberation struggles. But in either case, the hybrid model of equality (which Rossi used primarily in the context of women's liberation)

... anticipates a society in which the lives of men and whites will be different, not only women and blacks . . . the values many young men and women subscribe to today are congenial to the hybrid model of equality: the desire for a more meaningful sense of community, a greater depth of personal relations across class, sex and racial lines; a stress on human fellowship and individual scope for creativity rather than merely rationality and efficiency in our bureaucracies; heightened interest in the humanities and the social sciences from an articulated value-base; a social-responsibility commitment to medicine and law rather than a thirst for status and high income (Milner, 1970).

Rossi and Milner are suggesting that both the oppressors and the oppressed need to realize that the ultimate issue is not simply the redistribution or material goods and decision-making power, but rather a reordering of North American values to ensure that each person's needs for fellowship and creativity are also met. Indeed, Rossi suggests that competition for merely material resources (important though they are) is often a desperate attempt to fill a void whose real cause is the need for a sense of belonging and personal growth—a need which would be best satisfied by increasing interpersonal cooperation and communication.

The above comments are not those of persons at the heart of radical liberation struggles, but come rather from social science scholars observing current trends and hypothesizing their future direction. Are they naive in their optimism? To the ordinary observer, it might seem impossible that the various liberation movements, each apparently so intent on its own gains, might be moving towards a common goal like the one described by Milner. And yet, there is abundant evidence that the perhaps once parallel paths of Black Power, Red Power, women's liberation, gay liberation, *La Causa*, and all other movements are more recently seen by their respective members as part of a common metastruggle which can only be described as an insistence, in the end, on the kind of "people's liberation" espoused by Rossi in her hybrid model of equality.

Bibliography

Adams, J. Stacey: "Inequity in Social Exchange," in Leonard Berkowitz
(ed.); *Advances in Experimental Social Psychology*, Academic Press,
New York, 1965

Adorno, T. W., E. Frenkel-Brunswick, D. J. Levinson, and R. N. Sanford:
The Authoritarian Personality, Harper & Row, New York, 1950.

Allport, Gordon: *The Nature of Prejudice*, Addison-Wesley, Reading,
Mass., 1954.

——: *Pattern and Growth in Personality*, Holt, Rinehart and Winston,
New York, 1961.

——, and L. J. Postman: *The Psychology of Rumor*, Henry Holt, New
York, 1947.

Amir, Y.: "Contact Hypothesis in Ethnic Relations," *Psychological
Bulletin*, 71:319-342, 1969.

Aronson, Elliot and Vernon Cope: "My Enemy's Enemy Is My Friend,"
Journal of Personality and Social Psychology, 8:8-12, 1968.

Arthur, Ransom J.: *An Introduction to Social Psychiatry*, Penguin
Books, Baltimore, 1971.

Athey, K. R., J. E. Coleman, A. P. Reitman, and J. Tang: "Two Experiments Showing the Effect of the Interviewer's Racial Background on Responses to Questionnaires Concerning Racial Issues," *Journal of Applied Psychology,* **44**:244–246, 1960.

Bandura, Albert and Richard H. Walters: *Social Learning and Personality Development,* Holt, Rinehart and Winston, New York, 1963.

Barber, Theodore X., D. S. Calverley, A. Forgione, J. D. McPeake, J. F. Chaves, and B. Bowen: "Five Attempts to Replicate the Experimenter Bias Effect," *Journal of Consulting and Clinical Psychology,* **33**:1–6, 1969.

—— and M. J. Silver: "Fact, Fiction and the Experimenter Bias Effect," *Psychological Bulletin,* **70**:6, 1–29, 1968.

Bardwick, J. M. (ed.): *Readings on the Psychology of Women,* Harper & Row, New York, 1972.

Bart, Pauline, Personal Communication, 1971.

Baughman, Earl E.: *Black Americans,* Academic Press, New York, 1971.

Bayton, J. A.: "The Racial Stereotypes of Negro College Students," *Journal of Abnormal and Social Psychology,* **36**:97–102, 1941.

Beardwood, R.: "The New Negro Mood," *Fortune,* **78**:146, 1968.

Becker, H. S.: "Whose Side Are We On?" *Journal of Social Problems,* **14**:239–247, 1967.

—— (ed.): *The Outsiders,* The Free Press, Glencoe, New York, 1963.

Beez, W. V.: "Influence of Biased Psychological Reports on Teacher Behavior and Pupil Performance," *Proceedings of 76th Annual Convention of American Psychological Association,* **3**:605–606, 1968.

Bem, Daryl J.: *Beliefs, Attitudes and Human Affairs,* Brooks-Cole, Belmont, Calif., 1970.

——: "Self-perception: An Alternative Interpretation of Cognitive Dissonance Phenomena," *Psychological Review,* **74**:183–200, 1967.

Benney, M., D. Riesman and S. Star: "Age and Sex in the Interview," *American Journal of Sociology,* **62**:143–152, 1956.

Berger, Peter L.: *Invitation to Sociology: A Humanistic Perspective,* Doubleday, Garden City, New York, 1963.

Berscheid, Ellen and Elaine H. Walster: *Interpersonal Attraction,* Addison-Wesley, Reading, Mass., 1969.

Bettelheim, Bruno: "Individual and Mass Behavior in Extreme Situations," *Journal of Abnormal Psychology,* **38**:417–452, 1943.

—— and M. Janowitz: *Dynamics of Prejudice: A Psychological and Sociological Study of Veterans,* Harper & Row, New York, 1950.

Bird, Carolyn: *Born Female: The High Cost of Keeping Women Down,* David McKay, New York, 1968.

Blake, R. R. and J. S. Mouton: "Reactions to Intergroup Competition

Under Win-Lose Conditions," *Management Science,* 7:420–435, 1961.

Brazziel, William F.: "White Research in Black Communities: When Solutions Become a Part of the Problem," *Journal of Social Issues,* 29(1):41–44, 1973.

Brewer, Marilynn B.: "Determinants of Social Distance Among East African Tribal Groups," *Journal of Personality and Social Psychology,* 10(3):279–289, 1968.

Brickman, Philip and Donald T. Campbell: "Hedonic Relativism and Planning the Good Society," M. H. Appley (ed.), *Adaptation Level Theory,* Academic Press, New York, 1971.

Brink, W. and L. Harris: *Black and White,* Simon and Schuster, New York, 1966.

Bronfenbrenner, Urie: "The Mirror-Image in Soviet-American Relations: A Social Psychologist's Report," *Journal of Social Issues,* 17:45–56, 1961.

Broverman, Inge K., Susan R. Vogel, Donald M. Broverman, Frank E. Clarkson, and Paul S. Rosenkrantz: "Sex-role Stereotypes: A Current Appraisal," *Journal of Social Issues,* 28(2):59–78, 1972.

Bruner, E. M.: "Primary Group Experience and the Process of Acculturation," *American Anthropologist,* 58:605–623, 1956.

Bruner, Jerome S.: "On Perceptual Readiness," *Psychological Review,* 64:123–152, 1957.

Burton, R. and J. W. M. Whiting: "The Absent Father and Cross-Sex Identity," *Merrill Palmer Quarterly,* 7:85–95, 1961.

Byrne, Donn: "Attitudes and Attraction," Leonard Berkowitz (ed.), *Advances in Experimental Social Psychology, IV,* Academic Press, New York, 1969, pp. 35–89.

—— and T. J. Wong: "Racial Prejudice, Interpersonal Attraction, and Assumed Dissimilarity of Attitudes," *Journal of Abnormal and Social Psychology,* 65:246–253, 1962.

Cade, Toni: "On the Issue of Roles," Tom Cade (ed.), *The Black Woman: An Anthology,* New American Library, New York, 1970.

Campbell, Angus and H. Schuman: *Racial Attitudes in Fifteen American Cities,* Institute for Social Research, Ann Arbor, Mich., 1969.

Campbell, Donald T.: "Distinguishing Differences of Perception from Failures of Communication in Cross-Cultural Studies," F. S. C. Northrop and H. H. Livingston (eds.), *Cross-cultural Understanding: Epistemology in Anthropology,* Harper & Row, New York, 1964.

——: "Natural Selection as an Epistemological Model," R. Narol and R. Cohen (eds.), *A Handbook of Method in Cultural Anthropology*, The Natural History Press, Garden City, New York, 1970, pp. 51-85.

——: "Objectivity and Social Locus of Scientific Knowledge," Presidential Address to Division of Social and Personality Psychology of the American Psychological Association, Washington, 1969.

——: "A Phenomonology of the Other One: Corrigible, Hypothetical, and Critical," T. Mischel (ed.), *Human Action: Conceptual and Empirical Issues*, Academic Press, New York, 1969, pp. 41-69.

——: "Stereotypes and the Perception of Group Differences," *American Psychologist*, 22:812-829, 1967.

—— and R. A. LeVine: "Ethnocentrism and Intergroup Relations," R. P. Abelson, E. Aronson, W. J. McGuire, T. M. Newcomb, M. J. Rosenberg, and P. H. Tannenbaum (eds.), *Theories of Cognitive Consistency: A Sourcebook*, Rand McNally, Chicago, 1968.

Canadian Broadcasting Corporation, National News, November 1972.

Cantril, H.: *Gauging Public Opinion*, Princeton University Press, Princeton, N.J., 1944.

Caplan, Nathan: "The New Ghetto Man: A Review of Recent Empirical Studies," *Journal of Social Issues*, 26(1):59-73, 1970.

—— and J. M. Paige: "A Study of Ghetto Rioters," *Scientific American*, 219(2):15-21, 1968.

Carmichael, Stokely and Charles V. Hamilton: *Black Power: The Politics of Liberation in America*, Vintage Books, New York, 1967.

Chambliss, William J.: "The Saints and the Roughnecks," *Society*, 11(1): 24-31, 1973.

Chesler, Phylis: *Women and Madness*, Doubleday, Garden City, New York, 1972.

Christie, R. E. and M. Jahoda (eds.): *Studies in the Scope and Method of the Authoritarian Personality*, The Free Press, Glencoe, Ill., 1954.

Clark, Cedric X. (ed.): "The White Researcher in Black Society," *Journal of Social Issues*, 29, 1973.

Clark, J.: *William Styron's Nat Turner: Ten Black Writers Respond*, Beacon Press, Boston, 1968.

Clark, Kenneth B.: *Dark Ghetto: Dilemmas of Social Power*, Harper Torchbooks, Harper & Row, New York, 1965.

——: "Group Violence: A Preliminary Study of the Attitudinal Pattern of Its Acceptance and Rejection: A Study of the 1943 Harlem Riot," *Journal of Social Psychology*, 19:319-337, 1944.

—— and J. Barker: "The Zoot Effect in Personality: A Race Riot Participant," *Journal of Abnormal and Social Psychology*, 40:143-148, 1945.

—— and Mamie P. Clark: "Emotional Factors in Racial Identification and Preference in Negro Children," *Journal of Negro Education,* 19:341–350, 1950.

Cleaver, Eldridge: *Soul on Ice,* Dell, New York, 1968.

——: "Tears for the Pigs," *The Humanist,* 29:6–8, March–April, 1969.

Codere, Helen: *Fighting with Property,* J. J. Augustin, New York, 1950.

Coser, Lewis: *The Functions of Social Conflict,* The Free Press, Glencoe, Ill., 1956.

Couchman, Ian S. B.: "Notes from a White Researcher in Black Society, *Journal of Social Issues,* 29(1):45–52, 1973.

Davidoff, P.: "Advocacy and Pluralism in Planning," *Journal of American Institute of Planners,* 31:331–337, 1965.

Davis, James A.: "The Campus as a Frogpond: An Application of the Theory of Relative Deprivation to Career Decisions of College Men," *American Journal of Sociology,* 72:17–31, 1966.

Deutsch, Morton: "A Theory of Co-operation and Competition," *Human Relations,* 2:129–152, 1949.

—— and M. E. Collins: "The Effect of Public Policy in Housing Projects upon Interracial Attitudes," Eleanor Maccoby, T. M. Newcomb, and E. L. Hartley (eds.), *Readings in Social Psychology* 3rd Rd, Holt, Rinehart and Winston, New York, 1958, pp. 612–623.

Dodwell, H. H. (ed.): *The Cambridge History of India, vol. VI, The Indian Empire, 1858-1918,* Cambridge University Press, London, 1932.

Dollard, John: *Caste and Class in a Southern Town,* Doubleday Anchor, Garden City, New York, 1937.

Durkheim, Emil: *Suicide,* J. A. Spaulding and G. Simpson (trans.), The Free Press, Glencoe, Ill., 1951.

Elkins, S. M.: *Slavery: A Problem in American Institutional and Intellectual Life,* University of Chicago Press, Chicago, 1959.

Fanon, Frantz: *The Wretched of the Earth,* Grove Press, New York, 1965.

Feshbach, Seymour and R. Singer: "The Effects of Personal and Shared Threats upon Social Prejudice," *Journal of Abnormal and Social Psychology,* 54:411–416, 1957.

Festinger, Leon: "Informal Social Communication," *Psychological Review,* 57:271–282, 1950.

——: "Motivations Leading to Social Behavior," M. R. Jones (ed.), *Nebraska Symposium on Motivation, 1954,* University of Nebraska Press, Lincoln, Nebraska, 1954b, pp. 191–219.

——: *A Theory of Cognitive Dissonance,* Stanford University Press, Stanford, Calif., 1957.

————: "A Theory of Social Comparison Processes," *Human Relations,* 7:117–140, 1954a.

Fiedler, Fred E., Terence R. Mitchell, and Harry C. Triandis: "The Culture Assimilator: An Approach to Cross-Cultural Training," *Journal of Applied Psychology,* 55(2):95–102, 1971.

Foa, Uriel G., Terence R. Mitchell, and Fred E. Fiedler: "Differentiation Matchings," *Behavioral Science,* 16(2):130–142, 1971.

Forward, John R. and Jay R. Williams: "Internal-External Control and Black Militancy," *Journal of Social Issues,* 26(1):75–92, 1970.

Freeman, Jo: "The Social Construction of the Second Sex," Michele H. Garskoff (ed.), *Roles Women Play,* Brooks-Cole, Belmont, Calif., 1971.

Friedan, Betty: *The Feminine Mystique,* Dell, New York, 1963.

Fromm, Eric: *The Heart of Man,* Harper & Row, New York, 1968.

Goffman, Erving: *Stigma: Notes on the Management of Spoiled Identity,* Prentice-Hall, Englewood Cliffs, N.J., 1963.

Goldberg, P.: "Are Women Prejudiced Against Women?" *Trans Action,* 5(5):28–30, 1968.

Goldstein, M. and E. E. Davis: "Race and Belief: A Further Analysis of the Social Determinants of Behavioral Intentions," *Journal of Personality and Social Psychology,* 22(3):346–355, 1972.

Golightly, C. and D. Byrne: "Attitude Statements as Positive and Negative Reinforcements," *Science,* 146:798–799, 1964.

Gorden, Raymond L.: "A Sample Cross-Cultural Communication Packet: Cross-Cultural Encounter in a Latin American Bank," unpublished manuscript, Antioch College, Yellow Springs, Ohio, n.d.

Gordon, T.: Notes on White and Black Psychology, *Journal of Social Issues,* 29(1):87–96, 1973.

Gornick, Vivian and Barbara Moran (eds.): *Women in Sexist Society,* Basic Books, New York, 1971.

Gouldner, Alvin W.: "The Sociologist as Partisan: Sociology and the Welfare State," *American Sociologist,* 3(May):103–116, 1968.

Greenglass, Esther and V. Mary Stewart: "The Under-representation of Women in Social Psychological Research," *Ontario Psychologist,* 5(2):21–29, 1973.

Greenhaus, D.: "A Female Impersonator: A Photo Essay, *Society,* 11:(1):52–54, 1973.

Grier, William H. and P. M. Cobbs: *Black Rage,* Basic Books, New York, 1968.

Griffin, J. H.: *Black like Me,* American Library (Signet), New York, 1962.

Guilford, J. P.: *Personality*, McGraw-Hill, New York, 1959.

Gurin, P., G. Gurin, R. Lao, and M. Beattie: "Internal-External Control in the Motivational Dynamics of Negro Youth," *Journal of Social Issues*, 25(3):29–54, 1969.

Hacker, Helen M.: "Women as a Minority Group," *Social Forces*, 30(1):60–68, October, 1951.

Haney, C., C. Banks, and P. Zimbardo: "Interpersonal Dynamics in a Simulated Prison," Stanford University, Palo Alto, Calif., n.d. (Mimeographed.)

Hastorf, A. H. and H. Cantril: "They Saw a Game: A Case Study," *Journal of Abnormal and Social Psychology*, 49:129–134, 1954.

Heider, Fritz: *The Psychology of Interpersonal Relations*, Wiley, New York, 1958.

Henley, Nancy M.: "The Politics of Touch," Paper given at the American Psychological Association Convention, Miami, Fla., 1970.

Hill, J.: *The London (Ontario) Free Press*, February 25, 1970, p. 12.

Homans, George C.: *The Human Group*, Harcourt Brace, and World, New York, 1950.

———: *Social Behavior: Its Elementary Forms*, Harcourt Brace, and World, New York, 1961.

Horner, Matina: "Femininity and Successful Achievement: A Basic Inconsistency," M. H. Garskoff (ed.), *Roles Women Play*, Brooks-Cole, Belmont, Calif., 1971.

Howard, J. R.: "The Road to Huelga," J. R. Howard (ed.), *Awakening Minorities*, Aldine, New York, 1970.

Hughes, Everret C.: "Dilemmas and Contradictions of Status," E. C. Hughes (ed.) *Men and Their Work*, The Free Press, Glencoe, Ill., 1958.

———: "Good People and Dirty Work" *Social Problems*, 10(1):3–11, 1962.

Hughes, Everrett C.: "Good People and Dirty Work" H. S. Becker (ed.), *The Other Side*, The Free Press, Glencoe, New York, 1964, p. 23.

Hunt, J. McV.: "Has Compensatory Education Failed? Has It Been Attempted?" *Harvard Educational Review*, 39:279–300, 1969.

Hyman, H. H.: "The Psychology of Status," *Archives of Psychology*, 38(269):5–94, 1942.

Jack, Harold: "Native Alliance for Red Power," Wabageshig (ed.), *The Only Good Indian*, New Press, Toronto, 1970.

Jackson, G.: *Soledad Brother: The Prison Letters of George Jackson*, Bantam Books, New York, 1970.

Jeeves, Malcolm: *Scientific Psychology and Christian Belief*, Intervarsity Fellowship, London, 1967.

Jencks, C. et al.: *Inequality: A Reassessment of the Effect of Family and Schooling in America,* Basic Books, New York, 1972.

Jensen, A. R.: "How Much Can We Boost I.Q. and Scholastic Achievement?" *Harvard Educational Review,* 39:1–124, 1969.

Johnson, T. J., R. Feigenbaum, and M. Wiebly: "Some Determinants and Consequences of the Teacher's Perception of Causation," *Journal of Educational Psychology,* 55:237–246, 1964.

Jones, Edward E., K. E. Davis, and K. J. Gergen: "Role Playing Variations and Their Informational Value for Person Perception," *Journal of Abnormal and Social Psychology,* 63:302–310, 1961.

—— and H. B. Gerard: *Foundations of Social Psychology,* Wiley, New York, 1967.

Jones, J.M.: *Prejudice and Racism,* Addison-Wesley, Reading, Mass., 1972.

Jorgensen, Carl, C.: "I. Q. Tests and Their Educational Supporters," *Journal of Social Issues,* 29(1):33–40, 1973.

Jose, J. and J. J. Cody: "Teacher-Pupil Interaction as It Relates to Attempted Changes in Teacher Expectancy of Academic Ability and Achievement," *American Educational Research Journal,* 8(1): 39–49, 1971.

Julian, J. W., D. W. Bishop, and F. E. Fiedler: "Quasi-Therapeutic Effects of Intergroup Competition," *Journal of Personality and Social Psychology,* 3:321–327, 1966.

Kagan, J. S.: "Inadequate Evidence and Illogical Conclusions," *Harvard Educational Review,* 39:274–277, 1969.

Kariuki, Josiah M.: *Mau Mau Detainee,* Penguin Books, Baltimore, 1964.

Katz, D.: "Do Interviewers Bias Poll Results?" *Public Opinion Quarterly,* 6:248–268, 1942.

Katz, Irwin, Edgar G. Epps, and L. J. Axelson.: "Effect Upon Negro Digit-Symbol Performance of Anticipated Comparison with Whites and with Other Negroes," *Journal of Abnormal and Social Psychology,* 69:77–83, 1964.

Kepka, Edward J. and Philip Brickman: "Consistency Versus Discrepancy as Clues in the Attribution of Intelligence and Motivation," *Journal of Personality and Social Psychology,* 20(2):223–229, 1971.

Kian, M., S. Rosen, and A. Tesser: "The Reinforcement Effects of Attitude Similarity and Source Evaluation on Discrimination Learning," *Journal of Personality and Social Psychology,* 27:(3)366–371, 1973.

Kipnis, David: "Does Power Corrupt?" *Journal of Personality and Social Psychology,* 24(1):33–41, 1972.

Land, Kenneth C.: "On the Definition of Social Indicators," *American Sociologist,* 6:322–325, 1971.

Land, Kenneth C.: "On the Definition of Social Indicators," *American Sociologist,* 6:322–325, 1971.

Lerner, M. J.: "The Effect of Responsibility and Choice on a Partner's Attractiveness Following Failure," *Journal of Personality,* 33:178–187, 1965.

Lessard, Susanna: "Gay Is Good for Us All," *Washington Monthly,* December, 1970.

Levine, R. A. and D. T. Campbell: *Ethnocentrism: Theories of Conflict, Ethnic Attitudes, and Group Behavior,* Wiley, New York, 1972.

McClelland, David C.: *Personality,* Holt-Dryden, New York, 1951.

Maccoby, Eleanor: "Women's Intellect," in S. M. Farber and R. L. M. Wilson (eds.), *The Potential of Women,* McGraw-Hill, New York, 1963.

Mackenzie, Barbara: "The Importance of Contact in Determining Attitudes Toward Negroes," *Journal of Abnormal and Social Psychology,* 43:417–441, 1948.

Majdalany, Fred: *State of Emergency: The Full Story of the Mau Mau.* First published by Houghton Mifflin, Copyright © 1963 by Fred Madjalany. Reprinted by permission of Brandt and Brandt.

Mann, J. H.: "The Effect of Interracial Contact on Sociometric Choices and Perception," *Journal of Social Psychology,* 50:143–152, 1959.

Mannoni, D.: *Prospero and Caliban: The Psychology of Colonization,* Praeger, New York, 1956.

Mauss, Marcel: *The Gift: Forms and Functions of Exchange in Archaic Societies,* Ian Cunnison (trans.), The Free Press, Glencoe, Illinois, 1954.

Mead, George H.: *Mind, Self and Society,* University of Chicago Press, Chicago, 1934.

Meichenbaum, Donald H., Kenneth Bowers, and Robert R. Ross: "A Behavioral Analysis of Teacher Expectancy Effect," *Journal of Personality and Social Psychology,* 13:306–316, 1969.

Memmi, A.: *The Colonizer and the Colonized,* Beacon Press, Boston, 1967.

Merton, Robert K. and A. S. Kilt: "Contributions to the Theory of Reference Group Behavior," R. K. Merton and P. F. Lazarsfeld (eds.), *Continuities in Social Research: Studies in the Scope and Method of "The American Soldier,"* The Free Press, Glencoe, Ill., 1950.

Miller, Neil E. and R. Bugelski: "Minor Studies of Aggression: II. The Influence of Frustration Imposed by the In-Group on Attitudes expressed Toward Out-Groups," *Journal of Psychology,* 25:437–442, 1948.

Milner, Esther: "The Implications of Fertility-Limitation on Women's Life Career and Personality," paper given at the New York Academy of Sciences, February 19, 1970.

Money, John and Anke E. Ehrhardt: *Man and Woman, Boy and Girl,* John Hopkins University Press, Baltimore, 1972.

Morgan, W. and Jack Sawyer: "Bargaining, Expectations, and the Preference for Equality over Equity," *Journal of Personality and Social Psychology,* 6(2):139-149, 1967.

Morse, Stanley and Kenneth J. Gergen: "Social Comparison, Self-Consistency, and the Concept of Self," *Journal of Personality and Social Psychology,* 16:145-156, 1970.

Murphy, Gardner: *Personality,* Harper & Row, New York, 1947.

Myrdal, Gunnar: "A Parallel to the Negro Problem," in *An American Dilemma,* Appendix 5, Harper & Row, New York, 1944, pp. 1073-1078.

National Advisory Commission on Civil Disorders: *Final Report of the National Advisory Commission on Civil Disorders,* 1968.

National Commission on the Causes and Prevention of Violence: *The Politics of Protest: Violent Aspects of Protest and Confrontation,* 1969 Staff Report submitted by Jerome H. Skolnick, Director, Chicago Convention.

Newton, Huey: "A Letter from Huey Newton to the Members of the Panthers on Women's Liberation and Gay Liberation," *Chicago Women's Liberation Union Newsletter,* September, 1970.

Park, Robert E.: *Race and Culture,* The Free Press, Glencoe, Ill., 1950.

Pascale, Linda and Louise Kidder: "Penalties for Role Reversals: As Seen in the Popularity Ratings for Aggressive Women and Passive Men," Paper presented at Eastern Psychological Association, April, 1973.

Pettigrew, Thomas, F.: *A Profile of the Negro American,* Van Nostrand, Princeton, New Jersey, 1964a.

——: "Negro American Personality: Why Isn't It Known?" *Journal of Social Issues,* 20:4-23, 1964b.

Polanyi, Michael: *Knowing and Being,* Routledge and Kegan Paul, London, 1969.

Prescott, Suzanne and Katherine Foster: "Why Researchers Don't Study Women: The Responses of 67 Researchers," unpublished study, University of Chicago and Illinois Institute of Technology, Chicago, 1972.

Pugh, R. W.: "A Comparative Study of the Adjustment of Negro Students in Mixed and Separate High Schools," *Journal of Negro Education,* 12:607-616, 1943.

Ransford, H. E.: "Isolation, Powerlessness, and Violence: A Study of Attitudes and Participation in the Watts Riot," *American Journal of Sociology*, **73**:581–591, 1968.

Riess, Albert J. Jr.: "The Social Integration of Queers and Peers," H. S. Becker (ed.), *The Other Side*, The Free Press, Glencoe, Ill., 1964.

Roberts, H. W.: "Prior-Service Attitudes toward Whites of 219 Negro Veterans," *Journal of Negro Education*, **22**:455–465, 1953.

Rohner, R. P. and E. C. Rohner: *The Kwakuitl Indian of British Columbia*, Holt, Rinehart and Winston, New York, 1970.

Rokeach, Milton: "Belief vs. Race as Determinants of Social Distance: Comment on Triandis' paper," *Journal of Abnormal and Social Psychology*, **62**:187–188, 1961.

—— (ed.): *The Open and Closed Mind*, Basic Books, New York, 1960.

—— and L. Mezei: "Race and Shared Belief as Factors in Social Choice," *Science*, **151**:167–172, 1966.

—— and S. Parker: "Values as Social Indicators of Poverty and Race Relations in America," *The Annals of the American Academy of Political and Social Science*, **388**:97–111, 1970.

——, P. W. Smith, and R. I. Evans: "Two Kinds of Prejudice or One?" in M. Rokeach (ed.), *The Open and Closed Mind*, Basic Books, New York, 1960.

Rosenhan, David L.: "On Being Sane in Insane Places," *Science*, **179** (4070):250–258, 1973.

Rosenthal, Robert: *Experimenter Effects in Behavioral Research*, Appleton-Century-Crofts, New York, 1966.

Rosenthal, Robert and Lenore Jacobson: *Pygmalion in the Classroom: Teacher Expectations and Pupils' Intellectual Development*, Holt, Rinehart and Winston, New York, 1968.

Rossi, Alice: "Alternate Models of Sex Equality," *The Humanist*, **29**:3–5, 16, 1969.

Runciman, W. G.: *Relative Deprivation and Social Justice*, Routledge and Kegan Paul, London, 1966.

Saenger, Gerhart and Emily Gilbert: "Customer Reactions to the Integration of Negro Sales Personnel," *International Journal of Opinion and Attitude Research*, **4**:57–76, 1950.

Sanford, Nevitt, and C. Comstock and Associates: *Sanctions for Evil: Sources of Social Destructiveness*, Jossey-Bass, San Francisco, 1971.

Savarkas, Vinayak D.: *The Indian War of Independence, 1857*, Phoenix Publications, Bombay, 1947.

Sawyer, Jack: "The Altruism Scale: A Measure of Cooperative, Individualistic, and Competitive Interpersonal Orientation," *American*

Journal of Sociology, **71**:407–416, 1966.

———: "Establishing the Right to Be Heard: The Development of a Program Takeover," Frances F. Korten, Stuart W. Cook and John Lacey (eds.), *Psychology and the Problems of Society*, American Psychological Association, Washington, 1970a.

———: "Relative Deprivation: A Politically-Biased Concept?" *Psychiatry*, **34**:97–99, 1971.

———: "Toward a Psychology with Conscious Values," *American Psychologist*, **25**(7), xii–xv, 1970b.

Schachter, Stanley: "Deviation, Rejection, and Communication," *Journal of Abnormal and Social Psychology*, **46**:190–207, 1951.

——— and Jerome Singer: "Cognitive, Social and Psychological Determinants of Emotional State," *Psychological Review*, **69**:379–399, 1962.

Sears, David O. and John B. McConahay: "Racial Socialization, Comparison Levels, and the Watts Riot," *Journal of Social Issues*, **26**: 121–140, 1970.

Seaver, Burleigh: "Effects of Naturally Induced Teacher Expectancies." *Journal of Personality and Social Psychology*, **28**(3):333–342, 1973.

Seeley, J. R., R. A. Sim, and E. W. Loosley: *Crestwood Heights: A Study of the Culture of Suburban Life*, Basic Books, New York, 1956.

Segall, Marshall H., Donald T. Campbell, and Melville J. Herskovits: *The Influence of Culture on Visual Perception*, Bobbs-Merrill, Indianapolis, 1966.

Senn, David J.: "Attraction as a Function of Similarity–Dissimilarity in Task Performance," *Journal of Personality and Social Psychology*, **18**:120–123, 1971.

Sherif, Muzafer: *Intergroup Conflict and Co-operation: The Robber's Cave Experiment*, University of Oklahoma, Institute of Group Relations, Norman, Okla., 1961.

Shibutani, Tamotsu: *Improvised News: A Sociological Study of Rumor*, Bobbs-Merrill, Indianapolis, 1966.

Shils, Edward A.: "Authoritarianism: 'Right' and 'Left,'" Christie, R. E. and M. Jahoda (eds.), *Studies in the Scope and Method of the Authoritarian Personality*, The Free Press, Glencoe, Ill., 1954.

Simmel, Georg: *Conflict*, Kurt H. Wolff (trans.), The Free Press, Glencoe, Ill., 1955.

———: *Conflict and the Web of Group Affiliations*, K. A. Wolff and R. Bendix (trans.), Free Press, Glencoe, Ill., 1955.

Singer, Jerome E.: "Social Comparison–Progress and Issues," *Journal of Experimental Social Psychology*, **2**(1):103–110, 1966.

Skinner, B. F.: *Beyond Freedom and Dignity*, Alfred A. Knopf, New York, 1971.

Soares, Louise M. and Anthony T.: "Age Differences in The Personality Profiles of Disadvantaged Females," *Proceedings of Annual Convention of the American Psychological Association*, **6**(1):163–164, 1971.

—— and ——: "Expectancy Achievement and Self-Concept Correlates in Disadvantaged and Advantaged Youths," *Proceedings of the Annual Convention of the American Psychological Association*, **6**(2): 561–562, 1971.

—— and ——: "Self-Perceptions of Culturally Disadvantaged Children," *American Educational Research Journal*, **6**:31–45, 1969.

Solomon, F. M., William Walker, G. J. O'Connor, and J. R. Fishman: "Civil Rights Activity and Reduction of Crime among Negroes," *Archives of General Psychiatry*, **12**:227–236, 1965.

Stein, D. D., J. A. Hardyck, and M. B. Smith: "Race and Belief: An Open and Shut Case," *Journal of Personality and Social Psychology*, **1**:281–289, 1965.

Stewart, V. Mary: "Raising the Self-Esteem of Black Children Through Curriculum Manipulation," unpublished master's thesis, Northwestern University, Evanston, Ill., 1970.

Stonequist, E. V.: *The Marginal Man: A Study in Personality and Cultural Conflict*, C. Scribner's Sons, New York, 1937.

Stouffer, Samuel A., E. A. Suchman, L. C. DeVenney, S. A. Star, and R. M. Williams; *The American Soldier, Volume I: Adjustment During Army Life*, Princeton University Press, Princeton, N.J., 1949.

Styron, William: *The Confessions of Nat Turner*, Random House, New York, 1966.

Terman, Leona M. and L. E. Tyler: "Psychological Sex Differences," L. Carmichael (ed.), *Manual of Child Psychology* 2nd ed., Wiley, New York, 1954.

The President's Commission on Campus Unrest: *Campus Unrest: The Report of the President's Commission on Campus Unrest*, ("Scranton Commission"), 1970.

Thibaut, John W. and Harold H. Kelley: *The Social Psychology of Groups*, Wiley, New York, 1959.

Triandis, Harry C.: "A Note on Rokeach's Theory of Prejudice," *Journal of Abnormal and Social Psychology*, **62**:184–186, 1961.

—— and E. E. Davis: "Race and Belief as Determinants of Behavioral Intentions," *Journal of Personality and Social Psychology*, **2**:715–725, 1965.

United States Department of Health, Education and Welfare, *Toward a Social Report,* 1969.

United States Department of Labor, Office of Policy Planning and Research, *The Negro Family: The Case for National Action,* March, 1965.

United States Public Health Service, *Television and Growing Up: The Impact of Televised Violence,* Report to the Surgeon General, 1972.

Van den Berghe, Pierre L.: *Race and Racism: A Comparative Perspective,* Wiley, New York, 1967.

Velikovsky, Immanuel: *Earth in Upheaval,* Dell, New York, 1955.

———: *Worlds in Collision,* Doubleday, Garden City, New York, 1950.

Walster, Elaine, "Assignment of Responsibility for an Accident," *Journal of Personality and Social Psychology,* 3:73–79, 1966.

—— and R. Walster: "Effect of Expecting to Be Liked on Choice of Associates," *Journal of Abnormal Psychology,* 67(4):402–404, 1963.

Weber, Stephen J., Thomas D. Cook, and Donald T. Campbell: "The Effects of School Integration on Academic Self-Concept and Achievement," Paper given at the Midwest Psychological Association, Detroit, May 1971.

Wheeler, Stanton and L. S. Cottrell, Jr.: *Juvenile Delinquency, Its Prevention and Control,* Russell Sage Foundation, New York, 1969.

White, R. K.: "Misperceptions and the Vietnam War," *Journal of Social Issues,* 22:1–156, 1966.

Zajonc, Robert B. and J. C. Marin: "Co-operation, Competition, and Interpersonal Attitudes in Small Groups," *Psychonomic Science,* 7:271–272, 1967.

Ziman, J. M.: *Public Knowledge: An Essay Concerning the Social Dimension of Science,* Harvard University Press, Cambridge, Mass., 1968.

Zimbardo, Philip, C. Haney, W. C. Banks, and D. Jaffe: "The Psychology of Imprisonment: Privation, Power and Pathology," Stanford University, Palo Alto, n.d., mimeographed.

Index

PSYCHOLOGY
AND THE PROBLEMS OF SOCIETY

Kenneth J. Gergen, Consulting Editor
Swarthmore College

Ashmore and McConahay:
PSYCHOLOGY AND AMERICA'S URBAN DILEMMAS

Kidder and Stewart:
THE PSYCHOLOGY OF INTERGROUP RELATIONS:
CONFLICT AND CONSCIOUSNESS

Pizer and Travers:
PSYCHOLOGY AND SOCIAL CHANGE

McGraw-Hill Book Company
Serving Man's Need for Knowledge*
1221 Avenue of the Americas
New York, N.Y. 10020

0-07-034545